_____

TO

_____

FROM

_____

DATE

Cleere Cherry Reaves

UNFILTERED

LIVING *raw, real, + redeemed* BY JESUS

DEVOTIONAL GUIDE

INTRODUCTION

HI FRIEND!

When I say friend, I hope you can hear the inflection and warmth in my voice—I really consider you a friend. I am so glad that you picked up this devotional guide. I believe in it so much, and I know God has big plans to meet you right where you are.

When I was talking to Jesus about what He wanted us to dig into, I kept coming back to this word: Unfiltered. The real version of you and me. I believe that now more than ever, especially in today's culture, it is vital that you and I fight to bring this version of ourselves to Jesus. There is a myth that perfection is possible, and that Jesus expects us to sort through our emotions before spending time with Him. I can't think of a more dangerous untruth. Friend, there is no way to properly sort through your emotions apart from God, the One who made your heart. Only He knows the weight of your sadness, the strength of your joy, and the tenacity of your frustration. As I was reading through Scripture, I was reminded of so many times when God's people have approached Him with unapologetic honesty. Every emotion under the sun is mentioned in the Bible. I was so encouraged by these stories and how God remains faithful to His people even as they betray Him. I pray that as you work through this guide—at your OWN PACE—you will discover that Jesus is always your safe space. In whatever season you are navigating, He will always provide the refuge that you need and the peace your spirit craves.

My prayer is that you and I would find the courage and faith to bring every bit of our real selves to Jesus so that we can experience the abundant life He longs to give us.

You are deeply loved, highly favored, and wonderfully made. That is irrefutable.

Coffee in hand, cozy blanket in tow, and a heart open to the whispers of grace, let us embark on the journey of authenticity.

xoxo,

Cleere

Contents

01 : What's In Your Hand?. 8

02 : Desperate for Deliverance 12

03 : When Your Calling is Confusing 18

04 : When You Are Discouraged by Your Weakness. 22

05 : The Weight of Grief. 28

06 : Distracted Martha or Distracted by Details 32

07 : Struggling with Doubt 38

08 : Purpose Over Pleasure. 42

09 : Crying Out for Hope 48

10 : Your Condition Isn't Your Identity 52

11 : Unfiltered, Unashamed, and Unstoppable 58

12 : Wishing for the Past. 62

13 : When God's Promises Feel Far-Fetched 68

14 : Surrounded, Sustained, and Safe 72

15 : Unveiling the Depths of the Heart. 78

16 : When Faith Stumbles and Rises. 82

17 : Tempted to Retaliate 88

18 : Facing the Call 92

19 : Positioned, Protected, and Promoted 98

20 : Depressed but Devoted 102

21 : Recharge, then Respond. 108

22 : Standing Firm in the Fire 112

23 : Called, Commissioned, and Championed 118

24 : Sin that Leads to Shame. 122

25 : When Tragedy Makes You Bitter 128

26 : Change of Heart 132

27 : Elevated to Serve. 138

28 : When Comparison Leads to Criticism. 142

29 : Starved of Perspective .148

30 : Willing but Afraid. 152

How do I use this devotional guide?

Let me first say this before providing specific directions—the truth of the matter is, however you utilize this devotional guide in the way that you find helpful between you and Jesus is perfect. If it draws you to Him, the work is good.

Each of the thirty entries includes the following:

"GET REMINDED OF TRUTH": Each entry includes a story or passage from the Bible that provides an example of what it means to be unfiltered. This varies from unapologetically sharing the gospel to vulnerably exposing weaknesses to expressing fear in certain situations. These specific instances help you realize that God has always desired your authentic self, even when it feels uncomfortable and hard.

"GET CANDID WITH CLEERE": Sometimes, hearing others think out loud about a topic or story helps your wheels start turning too. In this section, I hope that it feels like having a heart-to-heart conversation with a friend over coffee as you both agree to go to the deep end. It is time to get honest and serious about what the Word of God says. It is the only way to have a fulfilling life! I pray as you read this section, you find the freedom to process through what the Lord is depositing in you, however it sounds and whatever it looks like.

"GET REAL WITH YOURSELF": There aren't many things I love more than working through questions regarding Scripture, theology, and overall thoughts that pop up as we ask the question, "How do I love like Jesus while maintaining honorable boundaries that protect my peace?" These questions were created to help you marinate on the text, imagine Scripture in real time, recognize the personal invitation of the Holy Spirit, and make it intimate for your own faith walk. These are great to do in groups too!

"GET RENEWED IN PRAYER": Prayer is the game changer. I always say, "Knowledge informs; revelation transforms." I believe that through prayer and inviting the Holy Spirit into this study with you, God can uncover, unveil, and unleash His unconditional love on you in a brand-new way. Simple and practical, these prayers will remind you that your Maker knows you better than you know yourself.

"MORE SCRIPTURES TO CONSIDER": Scripture is living, breathing, and active. Having verses on hand is like having literal ammo for any battle you will fight. These are your bullets! As you arm yourself with the Word of God and let truth become your mental soundtrack, you will realize how priorities get in order, thoughts realign, and new strength is found.

INTERACTIVE ACTIVITIES/SURPRISE PAGES: Throughout the study, there are different games, challenges, and fun ways to engage your heart, mind, and spirit together. These help you apply the concepts you are learning and incorporate fun into the picture. This is a helpful break, and you'll be surprised at how a little exercise helps you think outside the box.

I believe that through this journey of diving into what it means to be "unfiltered" in a world that is consumed by curation, you will taste a new level of freedom, wisdom, adventure, and peace. You were created to be set apart—embrace it! Remove the pretense, forget the pretending, and forgo the polishing. The One who made the world stamped you and called you, "Mine."

Let His refreshing love meet you where you are as you show the world what it means to live from a posture of rest, acceptance, and grace. What a beautiful picture that would be! No filter needed. ☺

Proud of you. In your corner. Thankful for who you are.

LOVE,

Cleere

SCAN HERE FOR A
GROUP LEADER'S GUIDE.

GET REMINDED OF TRUTH

EXODUS 3:9-14 NLT

Look! The cry of the people of Israel has reached Me, and I have seen how harshly the Egyptians abuse them. Now go, for I am sending you to Pharaoh. You must lead My people Israel out of Egypt."

But Moses protested to God, "Who am I to appear before Pharaoh? Who am I to lead the people of Israel out of Egypt?"

God answered, "I will be with you. And this is your sign that I am the one who has sent you: When you have brought the people out of Egypt, you will worship God at this very mountain."

But Moses protested, "If I go to the people of Israel and tell them, 'The God of your ancestors has sent me to you,' they will ask me, 'What is His name?' Then what should I tell them?"

God replied to Moses, "I AM WHO I AM. Say this to the people of Israel: I AM has sent me to you."

EXODUS 4:1-5 NLT

But Moses protested again, "What if they won't believe me or listen to me? What if they say, 'The LORD never appeared to you'?"

Then the LORD asked him, "What is that in your hand?"

"A shepherd's staff," Moses replied.

"Throw it down on the ground," the LORD told him. So Moses threw down the staff, and it turned into a snake! Moses jumped back.

Then the LORD told him, "Reach out and grab its tail." So Moses reached out and grabbed it, and it turned back into a shepherd's staff in his hand.

"Perform this sign," the LORD told him. "Then they will believe that the LORD, the God of their ancestors—the God of Abraham, the God of Isaac, and the God of Jacob—really has appeared to you."

WHAT'S IN YOUR HAND ?

Moses repeatedly responded to God's call with a response that resembled, "Please don't pick me. You've overestimated who I am." Moses was aware of the abuse his people, the Israelites, had endured. He deeply feared Pharoah and didn't want to have to be the one to face him, especially with so many lives hanging in the balance. His insecurity was drowning out his ability to hear what God was really saying—"Moses, I Am!" In other words, God was fully aware that Moses felt too small, too weak, and too incapable to be the man for this job; however, Moses's life is a wonderful example of a powerful truth—God can use anyone to accomplish His will. His power is made perfect in weakness (II Corinthians 12:9).

Did you know that Moses classified himself as being "slow of speech and tongue"? The very weakness that was a root of insecurity for him became the thing God wanted to use to redeem His people. God also told Moses that his brother Aaron, who was a good speaker, could accompany him and help him when he felt afraid. This story reminds us that God not only uses our weaknesses to glorify His name, but that He also provides practical help along the way.

Wherever God is calling you, and whatever He is asking of you, let this story bring you comfort. You are equipped for the role. He is aware of your struggles. And His power is made perfect in your weakness.

GET REAL WITH YOURSELF

01   Why do you think God called Moses to lead the people when He knew that Moses struggled with his words?

02   When you read these verses in Exodus, what insecurity does it make you think of in yourself?

03   Do you allow others to help you in your weakness like Aaron helped Moses? Can you think of a time when someone was an "Aaron" to you or when you fulfilled this role for someone else?

GET RENEWED IN PRAYER

HEY JESUS,

Thank You for always listening to me when I pray. When I talk to You, I feel myself relaxing as I remember that You are already near. Will You help me remember this story of Moses as I respond to Your voice and discern what's next? Remind me that my weaknesses don't scare You, for that's precisely what You want to use to further Your Kingdom. Thank You for not getting frustrated with me when I reiterate my worry or tell You why I'm afraid—You already know what's on my heart and mind.

Thank You for providing people in my life who are strong where I am weak. Humble my spirit so that I can recognize and receive Your provision in these places. When there is someone around me who I can help encourage, strengthen, or support, show me.

Like Moses, sometimes my insecurities speak so loudly that I struggle to hear Your voice above them. Help me remember that You are the Great I Am. When I focus on You, I regain my footing and can respond in faith.

IN JESUS'S NAME, AMEN.

ISAIAH 41:10 NLT

"Don't be afraid, for I am with you. Don't be discouraged,
for I am your God. I will strengthen you and help you.
I will hold you up with My victorious right hand."

GET REMINDED OF TRUTH

MATTHEW 9:18–26 NLT

As Jesus was saying this, the leader of a synagogue came and knelt before Him. "My daughter has just died," he said, "but You can bring her back to life again if You just come and lay Your hand on her."

So Jesus and His disciples got up and went with him. Just then a woman who had suffered for twelve years with constant bleeding came up behind Him. She touched the fringe of His robe, for she thought, "If I can just touch His robe, I will be healed."

Jesus turned around, and when He saw her He said, "Daughter, be encouraged! Your faith has made you well." And the woman was healed at that moment.

When Jesus arrived at the official's home, He saw the noisy crowd and heard the funeral music. "Get out!" He told them. "The girl isn't dead; she's only asleep." But the crowd laughed at Him. After the crowd was put outside, however, Jesus went in and took the girl by the hand, and she stood up! The report of this miracle swept through the entire countryside.

GET CANDID WITH CLEERE

DESPERATE FOR DELIVERANCE

This story mentions two extreme moments of vulnerability—both for the synagogue leader who was desperate for his daughter's healing and for the woman who had been bleeding for twelve years. Notice how Scripture mentions that both people possessed unwavering faith that Jesus had the power to heal.

Sometimes, having faith in the face of dire circumstances seems crazy. This is the challenge vulnerability presents to each of us: Will we trust the character of God over the circumstances we are facing? This is why vulnerability sometimes feels scary and counterintuitive.

Think about how long a few months can feel when you're navigating a hardship. Now, imagine enduring it for twelve years. The woman in this story is a testament to how courage and faith can change our lives in a moment's time. Healing doesn't always happen suddenly, but for both the woman and the synagogue leader's daughter, faith made it possible.

Let these stories remind us that it is often the presence of desperation that allows for the presence of the Deliverer to do what only He can do.

GET REAL WITH YOURSELF

01   When something negative happens to you or someone you love, do you try to take matters into your own hands, or do you turn to God in prayer?

02   If you were the woman who had been bleeding for twelve years, do you think you would have had this same response to Jesus? Or do you think you would have stopped believing healing was possible?

03   What is something you've stopped believing for that you think God may want to revive?

GET RENEWED IN PRAYER

HEY JESUS,

Thank You for stories that help me see the power of courage and faith. Help me live with the same expectation of Your presence. Highlight anything that I am holding onto that's keeping me from pursuing healing. Illuminate any area of pride that might keep me from reaching out to You for help.

I know that Your Word is true and that You are still in the miracle-working business—that is Your nature! Help me bravely seek your healing like the synagogue ruler and the woman in today's Scripture reading. I don't want to conform to those around me based on what's comfortable.

Sometimes, I feel frustrated when I am having to endure hardship. I know that You understand. You weep with me, Father. You aren't angry with me for wishing my circumstances were easier; rather, You have given me the authority to see beyond where I am and speak with hope and joy over my future.

Remind me that You have the final say in my life. Refocus my eyes on You

IN JESUS'S NAME, AMEN.

II TIMOTHY 1:7 NIV

For the Spirit God gave us does not make us timid,
but gives us power, love and self-discipline.

GET INSPIRED:

Chapter Break Pause

*"Let Him into the
mire and muck
of our world.
For only if
we let Him in
can He pull us out."*

MAX LUCADO

GET REMINDED OF TRUTH

LUKE 1:26–38 NLT

In the sixth month of Elizabeth's pregnancy, God sent the angel Gabriel to Nazareth, a village in Galilee, to a virgin named Mary. She was engaged to be married to a man named Joseph, a descendant of King David. Gabriel appeared to her and said, "Greetings, favored woman! The Lord is with you!"

Confused and disturbed, Mary tried to think what the angel could mean. "Don't be afraid, Mary," the angel told her, "for you have found favor with God! You will conceive and give birth to a son, and you will name Him Jesus. He will be very great and will be called the Son of the Most High. The Lord God will give Him the throne of His ancestor David. And He will reign over Israel forever; His Kingdom will never end!"

Mary asked the angel, "But how can this happen? I am a virgin."

The angel replied, "The Holy Spirit will come upon you, and the power of the Most High will overshadow you. So the baby to be born will be holy, and He will be called the Son of God. What's more, your relative Elizabeth has become pregnant in her old age! People used to say she was barren, but she has conceived a son and is now in her sixth month. For the word of God will never fail."

Mary responded, "I am the Lord's servant. May everything you have said about me come true." And then the angel left her.

WHEN YOUR CALLING IS CONFUSING

Is there a greater calling than being the Mother of the Savior of the World? This was Mary's role—a virgin girl chosen to shepherd the life that would save all other lives. Mary felt the weight of this calling. We can hear the vulnerability in her voice as she responded to the angel who delivered the news of her miraculous pregnancy as she questioned, "But how can this happen? I am a virgin." Though there was no greater privilege than to serve as the mother of Christ, she was understandably terrified as she tried to comprehend the logistics of her pregnancy.

Mary's vulnerability proves that God is aware of our concerns as He leads us into a new season or purpose in life.

Isn't it interesting, and yet not surprising, that God would reveal to Mary that her relative, Elizabeth, would be walking this journey before her as she experienced her own miraculous pregnancy? When we feel weary while navigating life's detours, there is nothing like community and friendship to remind us of what is true. Sometimes, when we need a little courage, we draw strength and courage from those who have gone before us. As we see the rich fruit cultivated in the valley of their lives, we find strength to endure our own. Carrying Jesus was Mary's greatest joy, but much like many things in life, it surely came with its own set of worries and fears.

Let this encourage you deeply—don't worry how God is going to take care of the details when He leads you into a new season. He will make sense of every unknown in time. A heart utterly dependent on Jesus is a heart that will always know peace.

GET REAL WITH YOURSELF

01 Mary was a virgin, which meant that a miracle was the only explanation for her pregnancy. Do you think you would have believed her if she told you she was carrying Jesus?

02 What's a time in your life when you were given a task or assignment for which you initially wished you wouldn't have been chosen?

03 When was the last time you felt afraid or discouraged? Did you talk to Jesus about it?

GET RENEWED IN PRAYER

HEY JESUS,

Thank You for being consistent in who You are and how You love—You never waver, and Your character is the greatest safety net in this life. Sometimes, I get caught in my own head, worrying about what seems possible, or what is socially acceptable, and it keeps me from fully embracing Your calling. Will You help me with this? Help me be more like Mary, fully devoted to You and Your will, even when it doesn't make sense. Understanding is never a requirement for worship—I know this. Help me live it out.

As I enter this season in life, make me aware of the little blessings you are sending my way to affirm where I am and that You're with me. When I feel moments of doubt, help me bring them to You—You yearn to hear them, comfort me, and lead me back in the way of truth. Thank You for knowing that my reactions are often based out of insecurity, not an unwillingness to follow You. Sometimes, I just forget that You are always near, and that You have promised to never leave me alone. I'm grateful for that.

IN JESUS'S NAME, AMEN.

II TIMOTHY 1:9 NASB1995

[God] has saved us and called us with a holy calling,
not according to our works, but according to His own purpose and
grace which was granted us in Christ Jesus from all eternity.

GET REMINDED OF TRUTH

JUDGES 6:11–16, 39–40 NLT

Then the angel of the LORD came and sat beneath the great tree at Ophrah, which belonged to Joash of the clan of Abiezer. Gideon son of Joash was threshing wheat at the bottom of a winepress to hide the grain from the Midianites. The angel of the LORD appeared to him and said, "Mighty hero, the LORD is with you!"

"Sir," Gideon replied, "if the LORD is with us, why has all this happened to us? And where are all the miracles our ancestors told us about? Didn't they say, 'The LORD brought us up out of Egypt'? But now the LORD has abandoned us and handed us over to the Midianites."

Then the LORD turned to him and said, "Go with the strength you have, and rescue Israel from the Midianites. I am sending you!"

"But Lord," Gideon replied, "how can I rescue Israel? My clan is the weakest in the whole tribe of Manasseh, and I am the least in my entire family!"

The LORD said to him, "I will be with you. And you will destroy the Midianites as if you were fighting against one man...."

Then Gideon said to God, "Please don't be angry with me, but let me make one more request. Let me use the fleece for one more test. This time let the fleece remain dry while the ground around it is wet with dew." So that night God did as Gideon asked. The fleece was dry in the morning, but the ground was covered with dew.

WHEN YOU ARE DISCOURAGED BY YOUR WEAKNESS

Have you ever wanted to ask God the question, "Why do bad things happen when You promised You would protect me?" Take heart in this: you are certainly not the only one. Gideon was threshing wheat at the bottom of a winepress, grief-stricken over the state of his people and wondering if God had abandoned him. Listen to the vulnerability of his words when the angel finds him: "If the LORD is with us, why has all this happened to us?" It is comforting to read that even the heroes of the Bible sometimes felt this way, isn't it?

Sometimes, the overwhelming circumstances around us tempt us to believe that we aren't seen by God—or that

if He does see us, He doesn't care enough to change our circumstances. However, we see later in the story that God's eyes were always on Gideon and his people. Sometimes, to receive a miracle, we must first walk a path we never hoped would be part of our story. We see later that God used Gideon and his three hundred men to defeat the Midianites.

Even though Gideon asked God for sign after sign, God met him right where he was. He was tender with Gideon's fears, patient with his doubts, and reassuring of his concerns. This story reminds us that our fragility invites God to come to our aid in a powerful way.

GET REAL WITH YOURSELF

01 When was a time in your life where you felt unseen by God or wondered if He was still on your side?

02 What excuses do you find yourself using—such as Gideon's "my clan is the weakest in the whole tribe and I am the weakest in the entire family"—in your current season of life? What does this reveal to you about your trust in God in that area of your life?

03 Reflect on a time when Jesus showed up for you in a big way. Looking back on that time, are you now able to feel thankful for the fragility you felt?

GET RENEWED IN PRAYER

HEY JESUS,

Thank You for the stories in Scripture and the reassurance You give us within them. They help me remember that I am never alone in any doubt I have or struggle I face. Will You help me recognize my situation as a setup for Your faithfulness? Make me acutely aware of any area in which I am failing to trust You so that I can work it out with You. Remind me that You don't get frustrated by my need for assurance. Steady my heart when I am struggling with fear, anxiety, or shame.

You made my heart for communication with You—it is the invitation to a rich and meaningful life. So, help me bring my concerns to you, knowing that You already know every thought before I think it. You see the depths of my heart and You not only love me the same, but You also give me purpose. Like the angel that appeared to Gideon and called him "mighty hero," You call me forth into the person that You created me to be. Help me stand in agreement with what You say over me and my life.

IN JESUS'S NAME, AMEN.

Colossians 1:11 esv

Being strengthened with all power,
according to his glorious might,
for all endurance and patience with joy.

GET INSPIRED:

Chapter Break Pause

"There is no safe investment. To love at all is to be vulnerable. Love anything, and your heart will certainly be wrung and possibly be broken. If you want to make sure of keeping it intact, you must give your heart to no one, not even to an animal. Wrap it carefully round with hobbies and little luxuries; avoid all entanglements; lock it up safe in the casket or coffin of your selfishness. But in that casket—safe, dark, motionless, airless—it will change. It will not be broken; it will become unbreakable, impenetrable, irredeemable. The alternative to tragedy, or at least to the risk of tragedy, is damnation. The only place outside Heaven where you can be perfectly safe from all the dangers and perturbations of love is Hell."

C.S. LEWIS

GET REMINDED OF TRUTH

II KINGS 4:1–7 NIV

The wife of a man from the company of the prophets cried out to Elisha, "Your servant my husband is dead, and you know that he revered the LORD. But now his creditor is coming to take my two boys as his slaves."

Elisha replied to her, "How can I help you? Tell me, what do you have in your house?"

"Your servant has nothing there at all," she said, "except a small jar of olive oil."

Elisha said, "Go around and ask all your neighbors for empty jars. Don't ask for just a few. Then go inside and shut the door behind you and your sons. Pour oil into all the jars, and as each is filled, put it to one side."

She left him and shut the door behind her and her sons. They brought the jars to her and she kept pouring. When all the jars were full, she said to her son, "Bring me another one."

But he replied, "There is not a jar left." Then the oil stopped flowing.

She went and told the man of God, and he said, "Go, sell the oil and pay your debts. You and your sons can live on what is left."

GET CANDID WITH CLEERE

THE WEIGHT OF GRIEF

This woman was a widow with nothing left to her name, and the creditors were coming to take what was most precious to her if she didn't pay her debts—her two sons. Imagine her fear, knowing that she truly was dependent upon a miracle. Her only choice was to be vulnerable about her state of desperation as she cried out to Elisha for help. When he asked her what resources she had, she told him she only had a small jar of olive oil. His response was for her to make herself even more vulnerable by setting out to the neighbors' houses and asking for whatever jars they have available, taking as many as she could get. While her circumstances were not preferable, and her grief was great, this story sets the stage for the miracle-working power of God.

It feels scary when you find yourself in a situation wondering, "How will I go on? What if this doesn't get better?"

The very practical needs of this widow's family were more than provided for as every jar was overflowing with oil, creating enough to pay her debts and sustain them for the future. Because the widow was honest about her situation, her scarcity became the avenue for God's abundant harvest. The same is true about your needs—when you invite God to help you in your time of need, He shows up in the most unpredictable and miraculous ways.

GET REAL WITH YOURSELF

01　　Have you ever wondered if maybe the widow let go of her bitterness about her husband dying and her family having nothing, and that's why she received the miracle? Do you think bitterness or pride about what your needs really are keeps you from experiencing God's abundance in your life in any way?

02　　Elisha asked the widow, "What do you have in your house?" How does it make you feel to know that God can use even the smallest resource to meet your needs?

03　　Has there been a time where desperation was the doorway for deliverance for you or someone you love? How has grief drawn you closer to God?

GET RENEWED IN PRAYER

HEY JESUS,

Thank You for knowing exactly where I am at in this day, what I have on my mind, and what I need each step of the way. Peace fills my soul when I think about the truth that wherever I go, You are already there. Nothing is a surprise to You. Will You help me bring every need to Your throne? Free me from shame concerning my present struggles and fill me with hope for my future. Show me how to be honest about my situation in a way that invites Your power into my life. Thank You for this story about the widow and the oil—it is hard to fathom such provision, but I know that nothing is too hard for You.

When I feel discouraged by my situation, help me remember Your promises. When I feel the weight of grief heavy on my soul, lift my head and show me how to ask others for help, comfort, and strength. I trust You with my needs.

IN JESUS'S NAME, AMEN.

PSALM 61:1–3 ESV

Hear my cry, O God, listen to my prayer;
from the end of the earth I call to you when my heart is faint.
Lead me to the rock that is higher than I,
for you have been my refuge, a strong tower against the enemy.

GET REMINDED OF TRUTH

LUKE 10:38–42 NLT

As Jesus and the disciples continued on their way to Jerusalem, they came to a certain village where a woman named Martha welcomed Him into her home. Her sister, Mary, sat at the Lord's feet, listening to what He taught. But Martha was distracted by the big dinner she was preparing. She came to Jesus and said, "Lord, doesn't it seem unfair to you that my sister just sits here while I do all the work? Tell her to come and help me."

But the Lord said to her, "My dear Martha, you are worried and upset over all these details! There is only one thing worth being concerned about. Mary has discovered it, and it will not be taken away from her."

DISTRACTED MARTHA OR DISTRACTED BY DETAILS

I know that many of us have heard this story in the Bible, especially around the holidays when everyone is hosting gatherings. Often, Martha gets shamed for not focusing on what's truly important. It is true—Martha was distracted by the practical obligations and prioritized her to-do list over the opportunity to sit with Jesus. However, when reading this story, I can greatly empathize with Martha, can't you? It was her home, and people had to eat—what was she supposed to do? Perhaps the problem is that she let the weight of responsibility overtake her awareness that Jesus, the Great Provider, was sitting right there—in the flesh—and surely, He knew what needed to be done.

I love Martha's honesty because I think we can all relate. Sometimes, as we begrudgingly tend to life's list of commitments, we show up and then complain to God that others aren't doing their part. Frustrated that they are experiencing freedom and spending time the way that we wish we could, we cry out to Jesus, "Tell them to help me! This is unfair!"

And what do we see is the Lord's response? He meets us with compassion, calling us back to what matters most. He never wanted us to be so overwhelmed by our responsibilities that we are distracted from His presence in our lives. The peace, joy, and rest that is available with Jesus is always possible, even when the to-do list is calling our names. We can trust that He will multiply our time, direct our steps, and maximize our efforts. Ignoring reality is not the answer, but recognizing that divinity is in the room is the way to navigate all that reality asks of us.

GET REAL WITH YOURSELF

01   Is there something that distracts you from Jesus's presence in your life? This might even be a good thing.

02   Do you find yourself crossing things off your to-do list with resentment? Dig deeper into that.

03   Society would probably deem Mary lazy or aloof, but she was focused on what matters. Do you find it hard to let Jesus determine the order of how you tend to things because you adhere to the expectations around you?

GET RENEWED IN PRAYER

HEY JESUS,

Thank You for knowing all the swirling thoughts circling in my mind and stealing my peace—You are as near as my breath. Sometimes, I forget to take a step back and remember that everything is a gift. Stress has a way of turning my blessings into burdens, but You help me return to gratitude. Thank You for covering me with grace and allowing me to bring my complaints, jealousy, and worries to You. You yearn for me to be real with You; this exchange is how I invite you into the places in my soul that desperately need healing.

As I go about my day and make decisions about where to invest my time and my energy, show me any place that is out of order. Help me prioritize what lasts in eternity and let all else go. When details feel imminent or life presents an urgency, slow me down and remind me that You're in control. Thank You for reminding me that a relationship with You is exactly that—leaning in, learning what is truly love, and then living accordingly. Sitting at Your feet like Mary, I'm listening to Your voice.

IN JESUS'S NAME, AMEN.

LUKE 12:34 NIV

"For where your treasure is,
there your heart will be also."

Chapter Break Pause.

*"I have ... found that
the very feeling which has
seemed to me most private,
most personal and hence
most incomprehensible by others,
has turned out to be
an expression for which
there is a resonance
in many other people."*

CARL ROGERS

GET REMINDED OF TRUTH

JOHN 20:24–29 NLT

One of the twelve disciples, Thomas (nicknamed the Twin), was not with the others when Jesus came. They told him, "We have seen the Lord!"

But he replied, "I won't believe it unless I see the nail wounds in His hands, put my fingers into them, and place my hand into the wound in His side."

Eight days later the disciples were together again, and this time Thomas was with them. The doors were locked; but suddenly, as before, Jesus was standing among them. "Peace be with you," He said. Then He said to Thomas, "Put your finger here, and look at My hands. Put your hand into the wound in My side. Don't be faithless any longer. Believe!"

"My Lord and my God!" Thomas exclaimed.

Then Jesus told him, "You believe because you have seen Me. Blessed are those who believe without seeing Me."

GET CANDID WITH CLEERE

STRUGGLING WITH DOUBT

Jesus had just been crucified on a cross—beaten, humiliated, and hung to die. Thomas, one of Jesus's disciples, had witnessed countless miracles during His ministry. Now, he found it difficult to reconcile Jesus's power with His brutal death.

Thomas was struggling with doubt. When the other disciples came to Thomas with the good news that Jesus had risen from the dead, reason robbed him of his ability to see past what felt natural, logical, or possible. How could Jesus be alive when He so clearly had just been lifeless?

Thomas gets picked on for being such a doubtful person, but how often do we struggle with trusting God's provision, especially during times of heartbreak and struggle? This story reminds us that God isn't angry at us for our questions. After all, He already knows what's on our minds. Our Scripture reading today tells us that when Jesus met Thomas after His resurrection, He offered Thomas the proof his doubting heart needed, telling Thomas, "Take your finger and examine My hands." He met Thomas's unbelief with faithfulness and truth. God's desire for us, however, is to believe in what we can't see (Hebrews 11:1). Like a VIP backstage pass, faith in the unseen allows us to gain access to the strength, freedom, and hope found when we step outside the box of possibility and believe in the impossible.

GET REAL WITH YOURSELF

01   With which area of your life do you most struggle with trusting God? Why do you think that is?

02   What do you think motivated Thomas to say he wouldn't believe in Jesus's resurrection until he had physical evidence? Do you think this came from a place of pride? Fear? Talk about that.

03   Are you willing to look foolish to others to walk in faith as God has called you?

GET RENEWED IN PRAYER

HEY JESUS,

Thank You for being such a personal and intimate Savior. You didn't just save me on the cross; You save me every day, and I am so grateful. Despite all that You have done and all that You've proven about who You are, I sometimes find myself behaving like Thomas, doubting Your presence or Your miracles. Is it my fear that causes me to doubt or my pride that wants further proof? Give me clarity concerning these issues, Jesus. Help me recognize and surrender my unbelief to You—You can handle it. Thank You for letting me bring my doubt to You. You faithfully meet me where I am.

I want to be a person who speaks with bold faith, walks with strong confidence, and leads with heavenly authority because I know who my Father is—help me.

IN JESUS'S NAME, AMEN.

LUKE 1:37 NIV

*For no word from God
will ever fail.*

GET REMINDED OF TRUTH

Ecclesiastes 2:1–11 nlt

I said to myself, "Come on, let's try pleasure. Let's look for the 'good things' in life." But I found that this, too, was meaningless. So I said, "Laughter is silly. What good does it do to seek pleasure?" After much thought, I decided to cheer myself with wine. And while still seeking wisdom, I clutched at foolishness. In this way, I tried to experience the only happiness most people find during their brief life in this world.

I also tried to find meaning by building huge homes for myself and by planting beautiful vineyards. I made gardens and parks, filling them with all kinds of fruit trees. I built reservoirs to collect the water to irrigate my many flourishing groves. I bought slaves, both men and women, and others were born into my household. I also owned large herds and flocks, more than any of the kings who had lived in Jerusalem before me. I collected great sums of silver and gold, the treasure of many kings and provinces. I hired wonderful singers, both men and women, and had many beautiful concubines. I had everything a man could desire!

So I became greater than all who had lived in Jerusalem before me, and my wisdom never failed me. Anything I wanted, I would take. I denied myself no pleasure. I even found great pleasure in hard work, a reward for all my labors. But as I looked at everything I had worked so hard to accomplish, it was all so meaningless—like chasing the wind. There was nothing really worthwhile anywhere.

GET CANDID WITH CLEERE

PURPOSE OVER PLEASURE

Solomon was the wisest man to ever live, and these are his words: "But as I looked at everything I had worked so hard to accomplish, it was all so meaningless—like chasing the wind." I wanted to include this passage in Ecclesiastes because if we are all being vulnerable, I think we spend a lot of time wondering if we are making a difference and if we are making good use of our time. We want to live a meaningful life, but so often, we, like Solomon, devote much time to meaningless pursuits only to wonder why we feel empty, weary, or discouraged.

Solomon teaches us that there is no amount of wealth, accolades, or success that can guarantee us a meaningful life. Despite being the wisest man, Solomon made a lot of destructive choices. Jesus doesn't expect us to live a perfect life, or one that is empty. He wants us to understand that apart from Him, there is no purpose in anything we pursue.

Heed the advice of Solomon—understand that his words are not based on facetious sentiments but profound revelations discovered through attaining everything and still feeling empty. Time is the great commodity that strips everyone to their true intentions. It is important to ask ourselves what kingdom we are trying to build and who our life is about. Allowing time for self-assessment and real evaluation allows us to hold tight to what matters and let go of everything that doesn't.

GET REAL WITH YOURSELF

01 It is almost impossible to understand the magnitude of Solomon's wealth and all that he achieved. And yet, it was never enough. Do you find yourself struggling to find contentment in your own life?

02 With what temptation do you find yourself wrestling the most? How can you invite Jesus into that space?

03 Research reveals that one of the most common regrets people have is creating a life based on the expectations of the others. Do you tend to struggle with this too? What would it take for you to live intentionally?

GET RENEWED IN PRAYER

HEY JESUS,

Thank You for this truth that absolutely sets my soul free: Your patience never runs out on me. I know that You gifted me with certain talents and infused me with a desire to live a big and meaningful life. Sometimes, I misdirect my energy into trying to fit in, working to earn my value, or exhausting myself striving to please the people around me. I'm sorry for this. I know that You see me, You love me still, and Your redemptive power can transform me. Help me receive Your grace. Renew my mind so that I can recalibrate my life.

I long to be a person who is intentional with my time, kingdom-driven with my resources, and heavenly focused in every pursuit; lead me in this, Father. Help me live selflessly and humbly. Fill me with a quiet confidence that has nothing to do with my appearance, accolades, or affirmation. Nudge my spirit when my priorities are out of order and help me make time to reassess at every turn. When I get off track, remind me that You're not angry with me—You just want me to get back on course, fully devoted to You. I love You, Lord. Nothing matters without You.

IN JESUS'S NAME, AMEN.

I SAMUEL 12:20–21 NLT

"Don't be afraid," Samuel reassured them.
"You have certainly done wrong, but make sure now
that you worship the Lord with all your heart, and don't turn
your back on Him. Don't go back to worshiping worthless idols
that cannot help or rescue you—they are totally useless!"

GET INSPIRED:

Chapter Break Pause

"The strangest thing happens when what we have most wanted to conceal is brought into the open. We don't die. Instead, we often begin to heal."

JOHN ORTBERG

GET REMINDED OF TRUTH

LAMENTATIONS 3:17–23 NLT

Peace has been stripped away, and I have forgotten what prosperity is.

I cry out, "My splendor is gone! Everything I had hoped for from the LORD is lost!"

The thought of my suffering and homelessness is bitter beyond words.

I will never forget this awful time, as I grieve over my loss.

Yet I still dare to hope when I remember this:

The faithful love of the LORD never ends! His mercies never cease.

Great is His faithfulness; His mercies begin afresh each morning.

GET CANDID WITH CLEERE

CRYING OUT FOR HOPE

The book of Lamentations is filled with grief and deep longing for restoration. It is the account of Israel mourning as God turned His back on them in judgment for their idolatry, just as the prophets said that He would. Want to know something? It is known to be one of the least studied and mentioned books of the Bible because it feels heavy and hard. However, there is a reason why the book of Lamentations is so important and, honestly, relatable. There will be seasons in our lives when we just want to hang it up and quit. There will be moments when we recall the promises of God and wonder if He has fulfilled them for others but skipped over us. Scripture includes this book for good reason—lamenting is necessary.

Being honest with the Lord, both individually and within a safe community, is a pivotal determinant of our spiritual health and maturity. Facing our pain and heartache head-on is a practice that proves we trust God enough to heal it. We have permission to bring any and every insecurity, fear, or worry to God in prayer without condemnation or shame. It may feel messy and uncomfortable, but it is the first step toward healing. Mending our own hearts is not our responsibility, but making ourselves known to the One who does is essential. Let the book of Lamentations serve as an encouragement to us—navigating our emotions and processing our grief is never linear, but neither is progress. What really matters is that we bring it all to Jesus.

GET REAL WITH YOURSELF

01   Do you tend to avoid negative or hard emotions or face them head-on?

02   Do you think you provide a safe space for others when they need to work through their emotions or talk about things that are uncomfortable or painful?

03   What are some helpful things you can do to turn your mourning into dancing? Are there practical disciplines that help you open your heart to God during a painful season?

GET RENEWED IN PRAYER

HEY JESUS,

Thank You for being the friend that always listens. When I think about the fact that You are able to tend to all creation and yet address all matters of every heart, I am overwhelmed with awe. Thank You for keeping Your eyes on my life. Sometimes, in my grief, I begin to feel that You have forgotten me, but I know that You are working everything out for my good.

Help me remember that growth isn't linear and that sorting through my emotions is part of learning to be more like You. Give me courage to deal with the hard emotions and not run from what feels uncomfortable. Help me find security in who I am as Your child so that I can process my heart with others without fearing their rejection or judgment. The cloud of grief covering my life will soon lift, and I will feel the sun on my face once again—that is always true. Thank You for being my firm foundation, my peace in every circumstance, and my hope when life is hard. Here I am, Lord. I bring all of me.

IN JESUS'S NAME, AMEN.

PSALM 18:6 ESV

In my distress I called upon the LORD;
to my God I cried for help. From his temple he heard my voice,
and my cry to him reached his ears.

GET REMINDED OF TRUTH

LUKE 5:12–16 NLT

In one of the villages, Jesus met a man with an advanced case of leprosy. When the man saw Jesus, he bowed with his face to the ground, begging to be healed. "Lord," he said, "if You are willing, You can heal me and make me clean."

Jesus reached out and touched him. "I am willing," He said. "Be healed!" And instantly the leprosy disappeared. Then Jesus instructed him not to tell anyone what had happened. He said, "Go to the priest and let him examine you. Take along the offering required in the law of Moses for those who have been healed of leprosy. This will be a public testimony that you have been cleansed."

But despite Jesus' instructions, the report of His power spread even faster, and vast crowds came to hear Him preach and to be healed of their diseases. But Jesus often withdrew to the wilderness for prayer.

YOUR CONDITION ISN'T YOUR IDENTITY

I love the language used by the man with leprosy in this story: "Lord, if You are willing, You can make me clean." Great humility and faith were intertwined with each breath he took—the humility to understand that Jesus didn't have to prove Himself and the faith to trust that his condition was nothing for his Creator. This passage reminds us that vulnerability becomes power when we realize how much God has extended to us and the foundation of mercy that brought us life.

Jesus's response to this man? "I am willing." I wonder how many times we strive to attain more, hoping to receive His affirmation when all He ever required of us was to acknowledge our need, and that He has the power to heal us. During this time, lepers were outcasts, highly isolated, and considered disposable. This man's circumstances brought him to the Savior seeking help, transforming his identity from a person who suffered rejection to one who turned people's hearts to the Redeemer. The crowds who witnessed his encounter with Jesus knew that if Jesus could heal a leper, He could do anything.

GET REAL WITH YOURSELF

01 The leper wasn't ashamed to publicly beg Jesus for healing. Why do you think that was, and what can you learn from his example?

02 We don't know how long this man had this condition or how much he had to struggle, but we do know his illness had not been short-lived. Have you ever allowed frustration or bitterness over a long-suffered trial to keep you from seeking healing? Why or why not?

03 The story ends by saying, "Jesus withdrew to lonely places and prayed." The Miracle Worker Himself responded this way. God wants us to draw near to Him in prayer. What steps can you take to protect your time with God?

GET RENEWED IN PRAYER

HEY JESUS,

Thank You for this beautiful reminder that there is nothing You are not willing to do to help Your people when they humble themselves before You. This leper's story challenges me! When I see You, do I respond in awe? Do I get so caught up in the circumstances I am navigating, that I forget that You are a good and kind God? The truth is, Your grace in my life is a greater gift than I could ever deserve. And yet, You choose to come to my aid when I call. Show me how to invite You into every corner of my life. Remind me that You aren't constrained by time limits, societal standards, or the worries of the world; You hold them all. Reveal to me where I need healing. Help me ask for it with confidence, and when You respond, help me ponder Your kindness in my heart with gratitude.

IN JESUS'S NAME, AMEN.

PSALM 57:2 ESV

I cry out to God Most High,
to God who fulfills his purpose for me.

GET INSPIRED:

Chapter Break Pause

Psalm 139 NLT

For the choir director: A psalm of David.

1 O LORD, you have examined my heart
   and know everything about me.
2 You know when I sit down or stand up.
   You know my thoughts even when
   I'm far away.
3 You see me when I travel
   and when I rest at home.
   You know everything I do.
4 You know what I am going to say
   even before I say it, LORD.
5 You go before me and follow me.
   You place Your hand of blessing on my head.
6 Such knowledge is too wonderful for me,
   too great for me to understand!

7 I can never escape from Your Spirit!
   I can never get away from Your presence!
8 If I go up to heaven, You are there;
   if I go down to the grave, You are there.
9 If I ride the wings of the morning,
   if I dwell by the farthest oceans,
10 even there Your hand will guide me,
   and Your strength will support me.
11 I could ask the darkness to hide me
   and the light around me to become night—
12 but even in darkness I cannot hide from You.
   To You the night shines as bright as day.
   Darkness and light are the same to You.

13 You made all the delicate, inner parts of
   my body
   and knit me together in my mother's womb.
14 Thank You for making me so wonderfully
   complex!
   Your workmanship is marvelous—how well
   I know it.

15 You watched me as I was being formed in
   utter seclusion,
   as I was woven together in the dark of
   the womb.
16 You saw me before I was born.
   Every day of my life was recorded in
   Your book.
   Every moment was laid out
   before a single day had passed.

17 How precious are Your thoughts about me,
   O God.
   They cannot be numbered!
18 I can't even count them;
   they outnumber the grains of sand!
   And when I wake up,
   You are still with me!

19 O God, if only You would destroy the wicked!
   Get out of my life, you murderers!
20 They blaspheme You;
   Your enemies misuse Your name.
21 O LORD, shouldn't I hate those who hate You?
   Shouldn't I despise those who oppose You?
22 Yes, I hate them with total hatred,
   for Your enemies are my enemies.

23 Search me, O God, and know my heart;
   test me and know my anxious thoughts.
24 Point out anything in me that offends You,
   and lead me along the path of everlasting
   life.

GET REMINDED OF TRUTH

ACTS 4:8–22 NLT

Then Peter, filled with the Holy Spirit, said to them, "Rulers and elders of our people, are we being questioned today because we've done a good deed for a crippled man? Do you want to know how he was healed? Let me clearly state to all of you and to all the people of Israel that he was healed by the powerful name of Jesus Christ the Nazarene, the man you crucified but whom God raised from the dead. For Jesus is the one referred to in the Scriptures, where it says, 'The stone that you builders rejected has now become the cornerstone.' There is salvation in no one else! God has given no other name under heaven by which we must be saved."

The members of the council were amazed when they saw the boldness of Peter and John, for they could see that they were ordinary men with no special training in the Scriptures. They also recognized them as men who had been with Jesus. But since they could see the man who had been healed standing right there among them, there was nothing the council could say. So they ordered Peter and John out of the council chamber and conferred among themselves.

"What should we do with these men?" they asked each other. "We can't deny that they have performed a miraculous sign, and everybody in Jerusalem knows about it. But to keep them from spreading their propaganda any further, we must warn them not to speak to anyone in Jesus' name again." So they called the apostles back in and commanded them never again to speak or teach in the name of Jesus.

But Peter and John replied, "Do you think God wants us to obey you rather than Him? We cannot stop telling about everything we have seen and heard."

The council then threatened them further, but they finally let them go because they didn't know how to punish them without starting a riot. For everyone was praising God for this miraculous sign—the healing of a man who had been lame for more than forty years.

UNFILTERED, UNASHAMED, AND UNSTOPPABLE

This passage of Scripture takes place right after Peter and John heal the beggar by the Beautiful gate. This man, who was well known in the community, had been lame since birth. At the time of his healing, he was over forty years old. Can you even imagine?

When the beggar met Peter and John, he was not seeking healing; he probably felt as though his time had passed to ask for such a miracle. However, Peter and John had other plans. They extended their hands, and the man was instantly healed. You can see this same unashamed faith on display again when Peter and John are brought before the council members who are angry that they were proclaiming the name of Jesus.

Peter responded (verses 8–12) with bold assurance that the healing was not performed through human efforts, but through the power of Jesus. It is tempting to think of vulnerability as fragile, unsure, or emotional. This story, however, depicts vulnerability in a way that reveals how deeply Peter and John's hearts were connected to Jesus. Because of their love for Him, they were willing to risk their reputations and whatever consequence came their way as the result of the healing. Dependence on Jesus may feel risky at times, but it provides the surest authority and power on this side of heaven.

The obvious miracle in this story is the healing of the beggar, but I think Jesus loved Peter and John's faith and their response to the council, just as much. Their response left the councilmen speechless and without options for retaliation. Peter and John were men who had been redeemed by Jesus and they couldn't stay quiet—what a testimony to those watching.

GET REAL WITH YOURSELF

01 The beggar in today's reading didn't receive the monetary gift for which he was asking. He received something better—healing. When you face opposition or consequences, do you immediately shrink back or wonder if you're going the wrong way?

02 How do you tend to handle rejection? Do you take it personally?

03 Our Scripture reading tells us that Peter and John were "bold" when brought before the council. Would you describe yourself as "unashamed," or do you tend to dilute your speech regarding faith based on those around you?

GET RENEWED IN PRAYER

HEY JESUS,

Thank You for providing opportunities for me to receive Your love and respond to others out of that overflow. Reading stories like that of Peter and John's healing of the beggar by the Beautiful gate, I am challenged concerning my own interactions. Do I stop and see others? Do I respond compassionately, or do I tend to judge them? I yearn to have unapologetic, unashamed faith that stands firm on the unstoppable power of Jesus. Will You show me how to do that?

Thank You for the reminder that when I stand strong in who You are, You provide grace for me each step of the way. Your truth is all I need. Remind me of this when others disagree, opposition strikes, or I feel discouraged by my circumstances.

Miracles happen in, around, and through me when I take You at Your Word. Help me do this so that I don't miss a single opportunity to witness Your power in action.

IN JESUS'S NAME, AMEN.

II CORINTHIANS 6:11–13 ESV

We have spoken freely to you, Corinthians;
our heart is wide open. You are not restricted by us,
but you are restricted in your own affections. In return
(I speak as to children) widen your hearts also.

GET REMINDED OF TRUTH

JOB 29:1–20 NLT

Job continued speaking:

"I long for the years gone by when God took care of me, when He lit up the way before me and I walked safely through the darkness. When I was in my prime, God's friendship was felt in my home. The Almighty was still with me, and my children were around me. My steps were awash in cream, and the rocks gushed olive oil for me.

"Those were the days when I went to the city gate and took my place among the honored leaders. The young stepped aside when they saw me, and even the aged rose in respect at my coming. The princes stood in silence and put their hands over their mouths. The highest officials of the city stood quietly, holding their tongues in respect.

"All who heard me praised me. All who saw me spoke well of me. For I assisted the poor in their need and the orphans who required help. I helped those without hope, and they blessed me. And I caused the widows' hearts to sing for joy. Everything I did was honest. Righteousness covered me like a robe, and I wore justice like a turban. I served as eyes for the blind and feet for the lame. I was a father to the poor and assisted strangers who needed help. I broke the jaws of godless oppressors and plucked their victims from their teeth.

"I thought, 'Surely I will die surrounded by my family after a long, good life. For I am like a tree whose roots reach the water, whose branches are refreshed with the dew. New honors are constantly bestowed on me, and my strength is continually renewed.'"

WISHING FOR THE PAST

If there was one person in the Bible who went through the ringer, and somehow, still walked the path of righteousness, it was Job. The suffering that he endured is too great to comprehend. In Job 1 and 2, we see that Satan recognized Job's wholesome nature and the purity of his heart and wanted to test him; and God let him. God allowed Satan to inflict immense pain and suffering upon Job as long as he spared Job's life. In this the passage above, you can see Job remembering what life was like before the tables were turned. Job had really tried to live righteously. In light of that, he couldn't understand why he was suffering. In his dismay, he said what many of us believe to be true: "Since I lived this way, surely ___ will be my life."

The book of Job details Job's struggle to navigate nearly impossible circumstances before finally coming to this realization: Despite how he felt, God was trustworthy. Despite what he thought his life was going to look like, he knew his God had not abandoned him.

Sometimes, I forget my relationship with God is not a rewards system. God's grace and favor are still present in my life even in hard times. The flipside of that is also true: I cannot live blamelessly enough to avoid suffering. Perhaps, as Job came to realize at the end of his life, there is good even in suffering if it brings God glory. Job's story also reminds us that it's okay to dislike our current circumstances or wish we could return to happier times. When we feel this way, the Comforter reminds us that He alone is our source of safety. God isn't unaware of our pain. He doesn't expect us to love what's difficult. What He does expect, or hope for, is that our love for Him continues to grow—no matter our circumstances.

GET REAL WITH YOURSELF

01   Do you find yourself wishing that you could go back to simpler, easier times? Do you think it's easy to romanticize the past to avoid embracing the present?

02   Suffering is part of the Christian walk—it can be self-induced, but it often has nothing to do with our decisions. If you are associating hardship with evil, then what does that say about the nature of God, particularly concerning His grace for us?

03   Who is someone in your life who has endured intense hardship and still chosen to praise God anyway? How have you seen their brave choice serve as a blessing to others?

GET RENEWED IN PRAYER

HEY JESUS,

Thank You for being honest about the truth that hardship and suffering are part of life here on earth. I know that heaven is my true home. Will You remove the word "unfair" from my vocabulary and help me remember the immense grace I have already received? Keep me from living in the pit of pity, despair, or worry.

Thank You for sharing Job's story with me. It teaches me to acknowledge my pain and turn to You for comfort.

Show me how to fully embrace the present and stop glamorizing the past. The moment I am living right now is good, and there is divine purpose here because You are leading me. You use every season to prepare me for the next. I am so grateful that my future is hopeful, even when the present feels dismal. Goodness, hope, and peace are possible here. Show me the way forward. May the warmth of Your friendship be my comfort and joy.

IN JESUS'S NAME, AMEN.

PSALM 94:19 NLT

When doubts filled my mind,
Your comfort gave me renewed hope and cheer.

Chapter Break Pause

*"Let us think of ways
to motivate one another
to acts of love and good works.
And let us not neglect
our meeting together,
as some people do,
but encourage one another,
especially now that the day
of His return is drawing near."*

HEBREWS 10:24–25 NLT

GET REMINDED OF TRUTH

GENESIS 18:3–15 NLT

"My lord," he said, "if it pleases you, stop here for a while. Rest in the shade of this tree while water is brought to wash your feet. And since you've honored your servant with this visit, let me prepare some food to refresh you before you continue on your journey."

"All right," they said. "Do as you have said."

So Abraham ran back to the tent and said to Sarah, "Hurry! Get three large measures of your best flour, knead it into dough, and bake some bread." Then Abraham ran out to the herd and chose a tender calf and gave it to his servant, who quickly prepared it. When the food was ready, Abraham took some yogurt and milk and the roasted meat, and he served it to the men. As they ate, Abraham waited on them in the shade of the trees.

 "Where is Sarah, your wife?" the visitors asked.

"She's inside the tent," Abraham replied.

Then one of them said, "I will return to you about this time next year, and your wife, Sarah, will have a son!"

Sarah was listening to this conversation from the tent. Abraham and Sarah were both very old by this time, and Sarah was long past the age of having children. So she laughed silently to herself and said, "How could a worn-out woman like me enjoy such pleasure, especially when my master—my husband—is also so old?"

Then the Lord said to Abraham, "Why did Sarah laugh? Why did she say, 'Can an old woman like me have a baby?' Is anything too hard for the Lord? I will return about this time next year, and Sarah will have a son."

Sarah was afraid, so she denied it, saying, "I didn't laugh."

But the Lord said, "No, you did laugh."

GET CANDID WITH CLEERE

WHEN GOD'S PROMISES FEEL FAR-FETCHED

Imagine being Sarah if you can—God has promised you that you would have a baby, but you have been unable to conceive children. Now you are old and gray, and God's promise to you feels far-fetched and impossible. Can you relate to feeling like you have somehow missed God's promise?

In Genesis 16, we see that Sarah tried to take matters into her own hands to have a child. Frustrated, she fought for control, but God was patient with her.

Sometime later, the Lord visited Abraham, ensuring him that Sarah would be pregnant within the year.

I love Sarah's reaction because I find it so highly relatable—silently laughing to herself, she reiterated the obvious: "I am old. Abraham is old. This is a joke." God responded to her fear turned laughter with assurance that He saw her and knew her heart, and that He was capable of anything. God was patient with her.

Sarah's story is a reminder that just because God's promises to us feel far-fetched, it doesn't mean He won't be faithful to keep them. Sometimes, the delay helps prepare us to receive the promise when it comes. That is what happened for Sarah. One year passed, and just as God promised, she gave birth to a son. And through that one child, Abraham and Sarah's family flourished for generations to come.

GET REAL WITH YOURSELF

01   How do you handle facing your weaknesses, spiritual shortcomings, and failures?

02   Sarah laughed at God's promise to her and Abraham, but her laugh was rooted in fear. When fear rises within you, how do you tend to react? Anger? Bitterness? White-knuckling for control?

03   Getting honest with yourself and God, do you feel like God failed to keep His promise to you or somehow overlooked you?

GET RENEWED IN PRAYER

HEY JESUS,

Thank You for always being so patient with me, even when I try to take control and take matters into my own hands. You see past my shortsighted desire to do it myself and realize that I'm clamoring to know that You haven't forgotten me. Give me the spiritual maturity to take a step back and remember that Your timeline knows no bounds. When You make a promise, You are faithful to deliver it, even when it feels far-fetched or impossible.

When, in my hurt, I am tempted to harden my heart, lead me back to Your tender care. Your eyes are always on my life, Your favor covers my weaknesses, and Your kindness carries me from one season to the next. Show me how to stand on Your promises and be an example to others. Thank You for letting me be candid about my fears. You restore to me the joy of my salvation and renew my heart with Your love.

IN JESUS'S NAME, AMEN.

HEBREWS 11:11 NLT

*It was by faith that even Sarah was able
to have a child, though she was barren and was too old.
She believed that God would keep His promise.*

GET REMINDED OF TRUTH

NEHEMIAH 4:7–15 NLT

But when Sanballat and Tobiah and the Arabs, Ammonites, and Ashdodites heard that the work was going ahead and that the gaps in the wall of Jerusalem were being repaired, they were furious. They all made plans to come and fight against Jerusalem and throw us into confusion. But we prayed to our God and guarded the city day and night to protect ourselves.

Then the people of Judah began to complain, "The workers are getting tired, and there is so much rubble to be moved. We will never be able to build the wall by ourselves."

Meanwhile, our enemies were saying, "Before they know what's happening, we will swoop down on them and kill them and end their work."

The Jews who lived near the enemy came and told us again and again, "They will come from all directions and attack us!" So I placed armed guards behind the lowest parts of the wall in the exposed areas. I stationed the people to stand guard by families, armed with swords, spears, and bows.

Then as I looked over the situation, I called together the nobles and the rest of the people and said to them, "Don't be afraid of the enemy! Remember the Lord, who is great and glorious, and fight for your brothers, your sons, your daughters, your wives, and your homes!"

When our enemies heard that we knew of their plans and that God had frustrated them, we all returned to our work on the wall.

GET CANDID WITH CLEERE

SURROUNDED, SUSTAINED, AND SAFE

The walls surrounding the beloved city of Jerusalem had been torn down and the people were exposed, vulnerable, and discouraged. Upon learning of this destruction, Nehemiah responded with deep emotion. Scripture says he sat down, wept, mourned, fasted, and prayed (Nehemiah 1:4). He cried out to the Lord and pleaded for favor with the King so that he could begin rebuilding the walls of Jerusalem. God answered his prayer, and Nehemiah and his people began rebuilding the walls.

The process was not without much opposition and many setbacks. Israel's enemies taunted, threatened, and hindered them. Nehemiah continually reminded the people of this: God would fight for them and grant them success in their endeavors. With unwavering faith and determination, Nehemiah and the people of Jerusalem persevered through the challenges. They worked tirelessly, each person contributing their skills and efforts to the reconstruction project. It is one thing to be exhausted and try to keep fighting for your own cause; it is a total other ball game to feel weary but be sustained by a larger mission.

Your raw emotion, real passion, and relentless love for others is a gift. Let this story remind you to fight for others rather than fight from fear. God is good with your unfiltered emotions and your opinions about how long, strenuous, and stressful the process can be. But as you lean in and remember God, you will find all that you need to keep going. Emotional strength is not the absence of discouragement; rather, it is the choice to keep building because you trust God's power and goodness.

GET REAL WITH YOURSELF

01   When you face opposition, how do you go about "remembering God" in the midst of battles?

02   Emotional resilience is the goal, but we often desire comfort more. Name someone you know who is emotionally resilient. What have they been through that allowed them to cultivate this trait?

03   What are you working on tirelessly today? Do you think your discouragement sometimes stems from getting caught up in the details of the process instead of prioritizing the bigger mission?

GET RENEWED IN PRAYER

HEY JESUS,

Thank You for Your Word and stories that help me remember how to remain strong and resilient in my everyday life. I know that there are many things in this life that will be like this wall of Jerusalem—where the process feels harder than I'd like, takes longer than I'd hoped, and includes more setbacks than I anticipated. As I build brick by brick, help me focus on what's important. When opposition strikes or the world around me tries to prevent me from completing the work You have given me to do, show me how to keep going. Victory is guaranteed when I keep You first and foremost.

In all that I do and say, lead me back to my "for." Remind me that my mission is so much bigger than myself; this infuses me with courage when I am afraid and reinvigorates my weary soul. Thank You for being gracious and tender with my complaints and weaknesses; You refresh me, reassure me, and give me the fortitude to keep fighting. I am confident in You.

IN JESUS'S NAME, AMEN.

I CORINTHIANS 13:7 NLT

Love never gives up, never loses faith, is always hopeful,
and endures through every circumstance.

HOW MUCH DO YOUR EMOTIONS DETERMINE YOUR DAY?

When you wake up, do you quiet your mind or open your phone?

Which practices do you currently do that support you talking to Jesus?

When you feel offended, what do you do?

Do you look to others to make you feel validated about where you are?

How do you handle it when things don't go your way?

Do interruptions frustrate you? Do you make space for them?

Do you feel burned out by life or unable to connect with others?

How do you reach out when you're struggling?

Do you allow margin and capacity to be a safe space for others?

Would you say you're responding or reacting to life?

GET REMINDED OF TRUTH

I Samuel 1:9–18 NLT

Once after a sacrificial meal at Shiloh, Hannah got up and went to pray. Eli the priest was sitting at his customary place beside the entrance of the Tabernacle. Hannah was in deep anguish, crying bitterly as she prayed to the Lord. And she made this vow: "O Lord of Heaven's Armies, if You will look upon my sorrow and answer my prayer and give me a son, then I will give him back to You. He will be Yours for his entire lifetime, and as a sign that he has been dedicated to the Lord, his hair will never be cut."

As she was praying to the Lord, Eli watched her. Seeing her lips moving but hearing no sound, he thought she had been drinking.

"Must you come here drunk?" he demanded. "Throw away your wine!"

"Oh no, sir!" she replied. "I haven't been drinking wine or anything stronger. But I am very discouraged, and I was pouring out my heart to the Lord. Don't think I am a wicked woman! For I have been praying out of great anguish and sorrow."

"In that case," Eli said, "go in peace! May the God of Israel grant the request you have asked of Him."

"Oh, thank you, sir!" she exclaimed. Then she went back and began to eat again, and she was no longer sad.

UNVEILING THE DEPTHS OF THE HEART

Hannah not only had to share her husband with another woman, but she herself was infertile. Her husband's other wife frequently taunted her about the fact that she couldn't conceive, tormenting Hannah until she was no longer able to eat. None of us can compartmentalize our hearts from our heads, no matter how much we would like to believe that is possible. Our feelings affect all of us. Hannah's deep emotional anguish stole her mental focus, physically affected her ability to eat, and spiritually drew her nearer to God.

Instead of walling up in self-protection or avoiding her intense emotions, Hannah went to the tabernacle to pray. She poured her heart out to the Lord and sought His comfort, His help, and His strength. She knew that she couldn't carry the weight of her sadness alone.

This story reminds us of something that is crucial to spiritual maturity: when we take our feelings to God, it becomes the invitation to greater intimacy with Him. Realizing our emotional capacity doesn't make us weak; it makes it possible for us to tap into the Father's strength. Not only did God meet Hannah in her sorrow, but He also provided the priest to encourage Hannah and speak life over her. In turning to prayer, Hannah's life was changed. She rediscovered joy and found strength to carry on. Later, she went on to have a son, Samuel, who became a prophet of God. Hannah's desperation led to her deliverance, which prompted her to dedicate Samuel to the Lord. How full circle is our Lord!

GET REAL WITH YOURSELF

01   When you pour out your emotions, do you tend to first seek help from others or from God? In challenging situations, how do you draw on your faith to find strength and guidance?

02   Scripture says that Hannah's joy returned long before she was able to conceive. Have you noticed how simply going to Jesus with your sorrows provides the peace for which you were searching?

03   God cares about your heart so much. Do you trust this? Do you think He sees your sorrow and feels it too?

GET RENEWED IN PRAYER

HEY JESUS,

Thank You for being such a kind and loving Father—I know that You care about every feeling I feel and every desire of my heart. Will You help me be like Hannah and bring all my cares to You? When my sorrow is great, help me surrender it to You. When I am afraid, give me Your peace. When I am frustrated, disappointed, or insecure, increase my awareness of Your presence. And along with these, help me bring my joy to You as well! Whatever I am feeling, I want to sort it out with You.

Thank You for reminding me that I am a whole being and I was designed this way on purpose. You don't expect me to operate separately from my feelings. You welcome all of me. Keep my eyes on You.

My heart is Yours, Father.

IN JESUS'S NAME, AMEN.

PSALM 51:12 NASB1995

Restore to me the joy of Your salvation
and sustain me with a willing spirit.

GET REMINDED OF TRUTH

LUKE 22:54–62 NLT

So they arrested Him and led Him to the high priest's home. And Peter followed at a distance. The guards lit a fire in the middle of the courtyard and sat around it, and Peter joined them there. A servant girl noticed him in the firelight and began staring at him. Finally she said, "This man was one of Jesus's followers!"

But Peter denied it. "Woman," he said, "I don't even know Him!"

After a while someone else looked at him and said, "You must be one of them!"

"No, man, I'm not!" Peter retorted.

About an hour later someone else insisted, "This must be one of them, because he is a Galilean, too."

But Peter said, "Man, I don't know what you are talking about." And immediately, while he was still speaking, the rooster crowed.

At that moment the Lord turned and looked at Peter. Suddenly, the Lord's words flashed through Peter's mind: "Before the rooster crows tomorrow morning, you will deny three times that you even know Me." And Peter left the courtyard, weeping bitterly

MATTHEW 16:17–19 NLT

Jesus replied, "You are blessed, Simon son of John, because My Father in heaven has revealed this to you. You did not learn this from any human being. Now I say to you that you are Peter (which means 'rock'), and upon this rock I will build My church, and all the powers of hell will not conquer it. And I will give you the keys of the Kingdom of Heaven. Whatever you forbid on earth will be forbidden in heaven, and whatever you permit on earth will be permitted in heaven."

GET CANDID WITH CLEERE

WHEN FAITH STUMBLES AND RISES

Peter had been close to Jesus throughout His ministry, witnessing miracle after miracle. Still, on the night of Jesus's arrest, Peter denied that he knew Jesus. Not once, not twice, but three times. As soon as he uttered his final denial, he remembered that Jesus had predicted his betrayal. Peter was brokenhearted by his own failure and wept. How could he? How could he deny the Savior?

Peter gets a bad rap, but to be honest, we all do this. Maybe not in such a tangible form as verbally denying our affiliation with Jesus but in the decisions we make and in what we prioritize. Scripture tells us in I John 4:8 that unless we love others, we do not know the Father. The failure to love is a struggle to which all of us can relate. Peter's story reminds us that anything that asks us to deny our devotion to Jesus will always leave us feeling empty.

I included the Scriptures from Matthew because it's so encouraging to see how Jesus transformed Peter's life; the man who denied that he knew Jesus became the Rock on which He later built the church. Take heart—however you may have struggled to remain faithful to Jesus, He is always faithful to love you through it and use you if you're willing.

GET REAL WITH YOURSELF

01   How do you think you struggle to represent Jesus?

02   Throughout Scripture, those who aligned with Jesus were continually rejected. Write about a time you were rejected for following Jesus, or a time you witnessed someone else being rejected.

03   When Peter denied Jesus, he was immediately reminded of Jesus's prediction of his betrayal. Write about a time you felt as if you'd betrayed Jesus. How did that feel?

04   Peter's transformation is incredible. How does this give you hope in your current season or situation?

GET RENEWED IN PRAYER

HEY JESUS,

Thank You for being such a forgiving and faithful friend. Even when I am fickle in how I operate or how I choose to love, You never waver from who You are. Like Peter, I sometimes struggle to remain faithful to You, and I am so sorry for that. Thank You for being patient with me and always reminding me of the truth. Help me to not fear rejection, judgment, or criticism from others. My job is to love them. You will do the rest.

Peter's restoration fills me with hope and increases my confidence in the plans You have for me. I know that You are capable of transforming, healing, and refreshing me, just like You did for Peter.

IN JESUS'S NAME, AMEN.

PSALM 103:4 NLT

He redeems me from death and crowns me
with love and tender mercies.

Chapter Break Pause

Seize this opportunity to inspire others! Cut out the cards on the adjacent page, and ask God who could use some encouragement. Keep them in your purse or pocket to share with someone in need. Slip one into a lunch bag or purse, and maybe even consider signing it with a message of prayer and support!

*I'm really proud
of you. I know this
season has not been
easy, but Jesus is
shining through you,
and His favor
is on your life.
Thanks for letting
me see Him work—
it inspires my faith!*

*Just a reminder:
if you ever need
a safe place,
I got you.
The big boulders?
I want to help
shoulder those!
It is a gift to me.
Love you.*

*Your willingness to
share how you feel
weak has allowed
me to see how strong
Jesus is through His
people. Thankful for
your bravery—it's
challenging me to
show up differently.*

*Light shines
greatest in the
darkness. God is
using this—keep
looking for His
fingerprints!*

GET REMINDED OF TRUTH

1 SAMUEL 24:3–10, 16–18 NLT

At the place where the road passes some sheepfolds, Saul went into a cave to relieve himself. But as it happened, David and his men were hiding farther back in that very cave!

"Now's your opportunity!" David's men whispered to him. "Today the LORD is telling you, 'I will certainly put your enemy into your power, to do with as you wish.'" So David crept forward and cut off a piece of the hem of Saul's robe.

But then David's conscience began bothering him because he had cut Saul's robe. He said to his men, "The LORD forbid that I should do this to my lord the king. I shouldn't attack the LORD's anointed one, for the LORD Himself has chosen him." So David restrained his men and did not let them kill Saul.

After Saul had left the cave and gone on his way, David came out and shouted after him,

"My lord the king!" And when Saul looked around, David bowed low before him.

Then he shouted to Saul, "Why do you listen to the people who say I am trying to harm you? This very day you can see with your own eyes it isn't true. For the LORD placed you at my mercy back there in the cave. Some of my men told me to kill you, but I spared you. ..."

When David had finished speaking, Saul called back, "Is that really you, my son David?" Then he began to cry. And he said to David, "You are a better man than I am, for you have repaid me good for evil. Yes, you have been amazingly kind to me today, for when the LORD put me in a place where you could have killed me, you didn't do it."

TEMPTED TO RETALIATE

David seems to have been a highly emotional guy. All throughout the book of Psalms, he expressed every emotion under the sun with eloquence and honesty. It seems likely that he often struggled to keep his emotions from overpowering his awareness of what is true, pure, and holy.

In this passage of Scripture, David must have certainly struggled with these issues. After all, he was on the run because Saul was after him, trying to take his life.

When given the opportunity to attack Saul, David refrained from harming him. He did, however, sneak forward to cut a portion of Saul's robe as evidence that he could have taken his life if he had chosen. He didn't do it because he knew this action was forbidden by God and that God chose Saul to be a leader during that specific time in history. This knowledge allowed David to humble himself and do the right thing, bringing glory to God. Of course, we all want to retaliate when we have been wronged. David's story teaches us that staying near to God helps us choose love over vengeance. What a lesson to us when we are tempted to seek vengeance. Like David, we can pause, pray, and trust God with those who have hurt us.

GET REAL WITH YOURSELF

01 Do you think it was a coincidence that David and his men ended up in the same cave as the very one Saul entered to use the bathroom? Or do you think God had bigger purposes at work? Explain.

02 Write about a time you were tempted to retaliate when someone hurt you, but you chose to listen to God's teachings instead.

03 Saul recognized David's humility and kindness. Ultimately, this was more of a learning opportunity for Saul than David. Write about a time God used your "tests" as a teaching opportunity for others.

GET RENEWED IN PRAYER

HEY JESUS,

Thank You for providing me with opportunities to experience emotion, pause in prayer, and remember that You want me to love others well. I know that when I have been hurt, my first impulse at times is to choose to retaliate. Thank You for helping me slow down and assess my situation from Your perspective. With Your help, I find patience for situations I previously couldn't navigate, and I see Your beauty in others, even when it feels hard or complicated. I am grateful for that.

In moments when hurt has clouded my judgement, help me see myself clearly. Show me where I have allowed bitterness to crowd out love. Heighten my empathy and remind me of the importance of practicing self-control. Thank You for the ability to manage my stress with You—discerning what is important, letting go of what isn't, and moving forward in kindness and peace. With each trial, I grow stronger, and I learn that honoring You is always what brings me joy.

IN JESUS'S NAME, AMEN.

MATTHEW 5:7 ESV

"Blessed are the merciful,
for they shall receive mercy."

GET REMINDED OF TRUTH

JONAH 1:1–5, 8–9, 11–12, 15–17 NLT

The LORD gave this message to Jonah son of Amittai: "Get up and go to the great city of Nineveh. Announce My judgment against it because I have seen how wicked its people are."

But Jonah got up and went in the opposite direction to get away from the LORD. He went down to the port of Joppa, where he found a ship leaving for Tarshish. He bought a ticket and went on board, hoping to escape from the LORD by sailing to Tarshish.

But the LORD hurled a powerful wind over the sea, causing a violent storm that threatened to break the ship apart. Fearing for their lives, the desperate sailors shouted to their gods for help and threw the cargo overboard to lighten the ship. ...

"Why has this awful storm come down on us?" they demanded. "Who are you? What is your line of work? What country are you from? What is your nationality?"

Jonah answered, "I am a Hebrew, and I worship the LORD, the God of heaven, who made the sea and the land." ...

And since the storm was getting worse all the time, they asked him, "What should we do to you to stop this storm?"

"Throw me into the sea," Jonah said, "and it will become calm again. I know that this terrible storm is all my fault." ...

Then the sailors picked Jonah up and threw him into the raging sea, and the storm stopped at once! The sailors were awestruck by the LORD's great power, and they offered Him a sacrifice and vowed to serve Him.

Now the LORD had arranged for a great fish to swallow Jonah. And Jonah was inside the fish for three days and three nights.

FACING THE CALL

Jonah's story will never grow old for me: "But Jonah got up and went in the opposite direction to get away from the Lord." What a statement to describe how the human mind works—maybe if I can physically go somewhere else, I can get away from God's plan, right? Jonah isn't alone in his hesitance to obey God when it is uncomfortable. God was asking him to go to a city and tell the people that God's judgment was headed their way because of their own poor decisions. It was the last thing Jonah wanted to do, so he hopped on a ship and headed in the opposite direction.

God chased Jonah. He sent a storm, and everyone was terrified, knowing that something far bigger than themselves was at work. Jonah knew better than to think he could sail away from his guilt. He confessed his disobedience to God and was thrown into the sea so that the storm would cease. In this transaction of events, those who were aboard the ship turned to God; He used Jonah's disobedience as the deliverance for others—what a Master!

Even in Jonah's direct disobedience to God, God knew that Jonah desired to be faithful. Though his fear had gotten the best of him, God's faithfulness saved him, refined him, and offered him another chance. How encouraging that the Father's patience doesn't run out on us; as He turns our mistakes into messages for others, He restores us to new life and purpose.

GET REAL WITH YOURSELF

01 Have you ever tried to physically relocate or somehow "run" from God and what you knew He was asking of you? If so, what made you run? If not, are there other ways you try to hide from God?

02 This storm was sent by God because of Jonah's disobedience, but others endured it too. Has there ever been a time in your life when you endured pain because of someone else's disobedience? Has your disobedience caused pain to others? Write about your experience.

03 Reflecting on Jonah's story and considering your own journey, what steps can you take to align your actions more closely with God's will? And how might facing discomfort head-on bring about positive transformation in your life and relationships?

GET RENEWED IN PRAYER

HEY JESUS,

Thank You for this unfailing truth: Your love never gives up on me. Even when I disobey, You remain consistent and patient with me. Help me learn from Jonah's story and practice obedience the first time.

When I feel guilt for doing the opposite of what You ask of me, give me the courage to change course. There is no point at which You will say, "You have gone one step too far." Your eyes are always on me, and Your arms are always open for me. When I choose to do the hard thing over the comfortable thing, I learn peace and the power of the Holy Spirit.

I know Your voice. Help me trust it, and follow it, wherever You send me. A life without peace is no life at all, and I can only know peace by obeying You.

IN JESUS'S NAME, AMEN.

PSALM 119:32 NIV

I run in the path of Your commands,
for You have broadened my understanding.

Chapter Break Pause

Seize this opportunity to inspire others! Cut out the cards on the adjacent page,
and ask God who could use some encouragement. Keep them in your purse or pocket
to share with someone in need. Slip one into a lunch bag or purse,
and maybe even consider signing it with a message of prayer and support!

*The raw,
real version
of you is my favorite.
I'm so grateful
for the way
God made you!*

*God has positioned
you, prepared you,
and promoted you
to exactly where you
are. You are ready
to shine for such
a time as this!*

*I'm thankful we
can both open up
about how we are
struggling. Always
know that I'm a call
away, I'll grab the ice
cream, and you're
never alone.*

*Big faith requires
big risks. I'm proud
of you for activating
your faith and falling
into the safety net of
Jesus—it's the safest
place to be!*

GET REMINDED OF TRUTH

GENESIS 39:2–4, 6–15, 19–23 NLT

The LORD was with Joseph, so he succeeded in everything he did as he served in the home of his Egyptian master. Potiphar noticed this and realized that the LORD was with Joseph, giving him success in everything he did. This pleased Potiphar, so he soon made Joseph his personal attendant. He put him in charge of his entire household and everything he owned. ...

Joseph was a very handsome and well-built young man, and Potiphar's wife soon began to look at him lustfully. "Come and sleep with me," she demanded.

But Joseph refused. "Look," he told her, "my master trusts me with everything in his entire household. No one here has more authority than I do. He has held back nothing from me except you, because you are his wife. How could I do such a wicked thing? It would be a great sin against God."

She kept putting pressure on Joseph day after day, but he refused to sleep with her, and he kept out of her way as much as possible. One day, however, no one else was around when he went in to do his work. She came and grabbed him by his cloak, demanding, "Come on, sleep with me!" Joseph tore himself away, but he left his cloak in her hand as he ran from the house.

When she saw that she was holding his cloak and he had fled, she called out to her servants. Soon all the men came running. "Look!" she said. "My husband has brought this Hebrew slave here to make fools of us! He came into my room to rape me, but I screamed. When he heard me scream, he ran outside and got away, but he left his cloak behind with me." ...

Potiphar was furious when he heard his wife's story about how Joseph had treated her. So he took Joseph and threw him into the prison where the king's prisoners were held, and there he remained. But the LORD was with Joseph in the prison and showed him His faithful love. And the LORD made Joseph a favorite with the prison warden. Before long, the warden put Joseph in charge of all the other prisoners and over everything that happened in the prison. The warden had no more worries, because Joseph took care of everything. The LORD was with him and caused everything he did to succeed.

POSITIONED, PROTECTED, AND PROMOTED

Reading this story, it's easy to think, "Man, Joseph really got the short end of the stick." This was not an uncommon theme in Joseph's life, as he was rejected by his own brothers and sold into slavery when he was young. However, there was also another thread that ran consistently through Joseph's life: God's favor which continually guided him from place to place, even amidst highly unfortunate circumstances.

In this story, Joseph's honor is inspirational. Joseph reminded Potiphar's wife that his master's trust and God's trust were his top priority. He could have remained bitter that he was a servant or that his family had put him in this position, but instead, he saw his current role as an opportunity to honor God. Even though this resulted in unjust punishment, the favor of God protected him, even in prison. Scripture says that because God was with him, He "caused everything he did to succeed." Joseph's life became a testimony to all: his family, Potiphar, Potiphar's wife, the prison warden, other prisoners, and townspeople. And now, you and me!

Joseph's story is a key lesson when it comes to vulnerability: when we commit to honor God, He will protect us and promote us wherever we go. This does not mean we won't experience unfair circumstances or difficult moments, but it does mean that when we do, we will never be alone.

01   Scripture says this about Joseph: "He succeeded in everything he did as he served in the home of his Egyptian master." His attentiveness to each role, rather than his eagerness to get ahead, was what prompted his promotions. How does this resonate with you?

02 Scripture says Joseph "kept out of her way as much as possible." Joseph saw danger and avoided it to honor God and position himself for success. How can you apply this principle to your own life?

GET RENEWED IN PRAYER

HEY JESUS,

Thank You for the way You filled the Bible with stories that help me gain perspective on my life. When I think about the road Joseph had to travel, it makes me realize how entitled, frustrated, or impatient I can get when I don't get my way or when things feel hard. Show me how to have an eternal perspective that recognizes Your goodness and Your provision in every space. Show me how to honor You right where I am. Help me stand firm in Your mercy when life seems to throw unexpected curveballs.

Give me wisdom so that I can make good decisions during stressful times the way Joseph did. Your favor is with me. Help me to remember that and trust that You will open the doors where, and when, I need them. Singing Your praises, I surrender to Your will for my life.

IN JESUS'S NAME, AMEN.

PSALM 84:11 NIV

For the LORD God is a sun and shield;
the LORD bestows favor and honor;
no good thing does He withhold
from those whose walk is blameless.

GET REMINDED OF TRUTH

JEREMIAH 20:7–18 NLT

O Lord, you misled me, and I allowed myself to be misled. You are stronger than I am, and You overpowered me. Now I am mocked every day; everyone laughs at me. When I speak, the words burst out. "Violence and destruction!" I shout. So these messages from the Lord have made me a household joke. But if I say I'll never mention the Lord or speak in His name, His word burns in my heart like a fire. It's like a fire in my bones! I am worn out trying to hold it in! I can't do it! I have heard the many rumors about me. They call me "The Man Who Lives in Terror." They threaten, "If you say anything, we will report it." Even my old friends are watching me, waiting for a fatal slip. "He will trap himself," they say, "and then we will get our revenge on him."

But the Lord stands beside me like a great warrior. Before Him my persecutors will stumble. They cannot defeat me.

They will fail and be thoroughly humiliated. Their dishonor will never be forgotten. O Lord of Heaven's Armies, You test those who are righteous, and you examine the deepest thoughts and secrets. Let me see Your vengeance against them, for I have committed my cause to You. Sing to the Lord! Praise the Lord! For though I was poor and needy, He rescued me from my oppressors.

Yet I curse the day I was born! May no one celebrate the day of my birth. I curse the messenger who told my father, "Good news—you have a son!" Let him be destroyed like the cities of old that the Lord overthrew without mercy. Terrify him all day long with battle shouts, because he did not kill me at birth. Oh, that I had died in my mother's womb, that her body had been my grave! Why was I ever born? My entire life has been filled with trouble, sorrow, and shame.

DEPRESSED BUT DEVOTED

Jeremiah was a wonderful prophet. He was bold in his prophecies for God, but he was also honest and vocal about his feelings of depression, loneliness, and struggle. Jeremiah was rejected by friends, punished by officials, and often found himself in difficult circumstances due to his unwavering commitment to delivering God's messages.

This passage interlaces praise with deep anguish; Jeremiah's deepest cries and most heartfelt feelings about the God he served are interwoven together. This can feel like it doesn't make sense; how could he feel so committed and joyous in one moment and feel so deeply saddened and grieved in the next? It was as though he was crying out about the weight that was on his shoulders while picking it up to put it back on again. Jeremiah's struggle reminds us that it is possible to feel joy and grief in the same moment. What a comfort it is to know that Jesus experienced the same conflict of emotions while on the cross. He endured unimaginable suffering in His physical body, but His heart remained fully committed to the work of redemption. Take heart when you experience the uncomfortable dichotomy of following Jesus; agony and anticipation have always been intertwined.

GET REAL WITH YOURSELF

01   Reflect on a time in your life when you experienced a mix of joy and grief. How did those emotions coexist, and what did you learn from that experience?

02   In what ways do you find comfort in knowing that even great prophets like Jeremiah and Jesus experienced the tension of conflicting emotions? How does this realization impact your understanding of your own emotional struggles?

03   Consider moments in your faith journey when you felt a weight on your shoulders, much like Jeremiah did. How did you navigate through those times? And how did your commitment to God's work influence your perspective?

GET RENEWED IN PRAYER

HEY JESUS,

I know that You listen to the cries of my heart as intently as You hear the praises of my lips. You know when something is hard or heavy for me before I ever come to You in prayer. Sometimes, I feel resentful or bitter for what You have asked me to give up or endure. I know that even suffering is mercy because it changes me to be more like You and rids my hands of treasures I won't get to keep. Though I know this, it still feels hard. You're okay with this. You just ask me to bring it all to You.

Will You show me how to look for joy, even when life is painful? Help me keep my mind on You. You are trustworthy in all that You say and do.

IN JESUS'S NAME, AMEN.

PSALM 23:4 NLT

Even when I walk through the darkest valley,
I will not be afraid, for You are close beside me.
Your rod and Your staff protect and comfort me.

GET INSPIRED:

Chapter Break Pause

Seize this opportunity to inspire others! Cut out the cards on the adjacent page, and ask God who could use some encouragement. Keep them in your purse or pocket to share with someone in need. Slip one into a lunch bag or purse, and maybe even consider signing it with a message of prayer and support!

Praying this with you: Hey Jesus, thank You for the way that You cover and protect me. I feel my anxiety peaking up some, but I know that Your hand is holding me. Lead me in the way of peace. In Jesus's name, Amen.

Praying this with you: Hey Jesus, if I'm being honest, I'm struggling. I feel a little overwhelmed and need Your help. Can You show me where to go, what to hold, and what to do? Give me clarity. Assure me that You will provide the whole way home. In Jesus's name, Amen.

Praying this with you: Hey Jesus, I am grateful for the way that Your mercy blankets my day and covers all my yesterdays. Show me how to maximize my day and fully receive Your grace—I'll never deserve it but my greatest gift to You is embracing the abundant life You've given me. In Jesus's name, Amen.

Praying this with you: Hey Jesus, thank You for being my refuge and my safe place in every season, amidst every struggle, and in every situation I will ever face. I am not afraid because You are with me. Your kindness is keeping me in perfect peace, and my mind is fixed on You. In Jesus's name, Amen.

GET REMINDED OF TRUTH

I KINGS 19:1–9 NLT

When Ahab got home, he told Jezebel everything Elijah had done, including the way he had killed all the prophets of Baal. So Jezebel sent this message to Elijah: "May the gods strike me and even kill me if by this time tomorrow I have not killed you just as you killed them."

Elijah was afraid and fled for his life. He went to Beersheba, a town in Judah, and he left his servant there. Then he went on alone into the wilderness, traveling all day. He sat down under a solitary broom tree and prayed that he might die. "I have had enough, Lord," he said. "Take my life, for I am no better than my ancestors who have already died."

Then he lay down and slept under the broom tree. But as he was sleeping, an angel touched him and told him, "Get up and eat!" He looked around and there beside his head was some bread baked on hot stones and a jar of water! So he ate and drank and lay down again.

Then the angel of the Lord came again and touched him and said, "Get up and eat some more, or the journey ahead will be too much for you."

So he got up and ate and drank, and the food gave him enough strength to travel forty days and forty nights to Mount Sinai, the mountain of God. There he came to a cave, where he spent the night.

GET CANDID WITH CLEERE

RECHARGE, THEN RESPOND

Tired and hungry—that's what Elijah was. He was weary from his travels and wayward in his thoughts. Elijah had faithfully served the Lord and stood against King Ahab, and he could physically take no more. His feelings were telling him to give up, that he couldn't sustain the journey. Then an angel came and reminded him that all he needed was time to rest and recharge.

How often do we confuse feelings with truth? Opposition comes, and we want to run away. Exhaustion hits, and we want to quit our day jobs. Sometimes, we must take a note from Elijah: lay down, be still, nourish our bodies and minds, and quiet our souls. After Elijah ate and rested, he was able to discern the whisper of God and continue in his ministry.

Verse four says Elijah prayed to die; verse eight says Elijah then traveled forty more days to the next place God was calling him to go. The difference was rest, renewal, and the presence of God. God understands when we are tired and weak; however, He does need us to recognize when it's time for a nap and some nourishment. He delights in helping us. He is compassionate when we are weary and renews our strength when we want to quit.

GET REAL WITH YOURSELF

01   It sounds silly but it's true: the enemy works overtime when you're tired or hungry. When have you seen this to be true in your own life?

02   Scripture says, "Then he went on alone into the wilderness." Do you think this was significant that Elijah was by himself? Why?

The angel said, "Get up and eat some more, or the journey ahead will be too much for you." This obviously shows that he knew what was ahead for Elijah. Do you think sometimes that you underestimate your physical needs and pay the price? Why or why not?

GET RENEWED IN PRAYER

HEY JESUS,

Thank You for the way that You know me so intimately and love me so unconditionally. Reading the story of Elijah makes me feel seen. This great prophet grew tired and weary on his journey and did not realize how much his body had been affected. Sometimes, my pride convinces me that my feelings are truth, but I know that You are so much bigger than how I feel. Thank You for slowing me down and reminding me that I often just need a nap and some nourishment.

Thank You for sustaining me. You will never call me somewhere without providing me with everything I need to get there and flourish. Remind me that common sense is my friend and awareness of my needs honors You; You find no glory in my overworking, overcompensating, or overdoing. Thank You for the fresh perspective and fierce strength I find when I rest in You. Your angels can handle what happens when I sleep.

IN JESUS'S NAME, AMEN.

PSALM 68:9 NIV

You gave abundant showers, O God;
You refreshed Your weary inheritance.

GET REMINDED OF TRUTH

DANIEL 3:19–28 NLT

Nebuchadnezzar was so furious with Shadrach, Meshach, and Abednego that his face became distorted with rage. He commanded that the furnace be heated seven times hotter than usual. Then he ordered some of the strongest men of his army to bind Shadrach, Meshach, and Abednego and throw them into the blazing furnace. So they tied them up and threw them into the furnace, fully dressed in their pants, turbans, robes, and other garments. And because the king, in his anger, had demanded such a hot fire in the furnace, the flames killed the soldiers as they threw the three men in. So Shadrach, Meshach, and Abednego, securely tied, fell into the roaring flames.

But suddenly, Nebuchadnezzar jumped up in amazement and exclaimed to his advisers, "Didn't we tie up three men and throw them into the furnace?"

"Yes, Your Majesty, we certainly did," they replied.

"Look!" Nebuchadnezzar shouted. "I see four men, unbound, walking around in the fire unharmed! And the fourth looks like a god!"

Then Nebuchadnezzar came as close as he could to the door of the flaming furnace and shouted: "Shadrach, Meshach, and Abednego, servants of the Most High God, come out! Come here!"

So Shadrach, Meshach, and Abednego stepped out of the fire. Then the high officers, officials, governors, and advisers crowded around them and saw that the fire had not touched them. Not a hair on their heads was singed, and their clothing was not scorched. They didn't even smell of smoke!

Then Nebuchadnezzar said, "Praise to the God of Shadrach, Meshach, and Abednego! He sent His angel to rescue His servants who trusted in Him. They defied the king's command and were willing to die rather than serve or worship any god except their own God.

GET CANDID WITH CLEERE

STANDING FIRM IN THE FIRE

This story is hard to understand: three men, Shadrach, Meshach, and Abednego, get thrown into the fiery furnace because they refused to worship King Nebuchadnezzar. Their loyalty to God was confusing and shocking to those around them: Did they not realize the torture that was about to take place? But as they were thrown into the fire to be punished, this became the very thing that made the king praise the one true God. The three men soon walked out of the fiery furnace without even smelling like smoke.

Shadrach, Meshach, and Abednego had a powerful perspective; they knew that the fire might be physically dangerous, but defying God was far more perilous for their souls. They determined that they would not let earthly consequences determine who they worshiped, and in turn, God protected them. Their testimony became an example to everyone, including the very king they defied.

It is not preferential circumstances that prove we trust God; it is the painful circumstances and the uncertain chapters of life that present us with the question: "Who do you really worship?" Clearly, Shadrach, Meshach, and Abednego feared God because they followed His way, even when threatened with the fiery furnace.

GET REAL WITH YOURSELF

01 Shadrach, Meshach, and Abednego could have just kept quiet and pretended to worship King Nebuchadnezzar, but they took God seriously. They knew they could never hide from the one true God. What would you have done?

02 These three men are included in Scripture because of their willingness to defy the king and stand firm in faith, but they still had to walk through the fire—literally. What does this tell you about painful seasons or hard times in your life?

03 The king's fury was rooted in pride. How does your pride tend to show up? What are some triggers for you?

GET RENEWED IN PRAYER

HEY JESUS,

Thank You for the constant clean slate You give me to be a person of courage and faith. Will You help me walk in the same bravery and trust that Shadrach, Meshach, and Abednego walked in? Remind me that fearing You will always be my best and greatest decision, no matter the consequences. You promise to never leave me during difficult times, and I know You will protect me.

Show me how to recognize moments of opposition and rejection as opportunities to display my trust in You. Great is Your faithfulness, Father. You are merciful and loving. No matter what I face today, I will remember this: I am not alone. You are with me.

IN JESUS'S NAME, AMEN.

Daniel 10:19 esv

And he said, "O man greatly loved,
fear not, peace be with you; be strong and of good courage."
And as he spoke to me, I was strengthened and said,
"Let my lord speak, for you have strengthened me."

Chapter Break Pause

Seize this opportunity to inspire others! Cut out the cards on the adjacent page,
and ask God who could use some encouragement. Keep them in your purse or pocket
to share with someone in need. Slip one into a lunch bag or purse,
and maybe even consider signing it with a message of prayer and support!

*Jesus is exactly
who He says He is.
You can trust
that in every space.*

*Jesus delights
over all of
who you are.
Let His love
be your banner.*

*Jesus is
the Tear Collector,
the Promise Keeper,
the Great Shepherd,
and the Wonderful
Counselor.
Sit with Him.*

*Jesus came to
redeem every lost
and broken thing.
He is the restorer
of time, hope,
strength, and joy.
Keep going.*

week five

DAY THREE

GET REMINDED OF TRUTH

ACTS 13:44–52 NLT

The following week almost the entire city turned out to hear them preach the word of the Lord. But when some of the Jews saw the crowds, they were jealous; so they slandered Paul and argued against whatever he said.

Then Paul and Barnabas spoke out boldly and declared, "It was necessary that we first preach the word of God to you Jews. But since you have rejected it and judged yourselves unworthy of eternal life, we will offer it to the Gentiles. For the Lord gave us this command when He said, 'I have made you a light to the Gentiles, to bring salvation to the farthest corners of the earth.'"

When the Gentiles heard this, they were very glad and thanked the Lord for His message; and all who were chosen for eternal life became believers. So the Lord's message spread throughout that region.

Then the Jews stirred up the influential religious women and the leaders of the city, and they incited a mob against Paul and Barnabas and ran them out of town. So they shook the dust from their feet as a sign of rejection and went to the town of Iconium. And the believers were filled with joy and with the Holy Spirit.

CALLED, COMMISSIONED, AND CHAMPIONED

Before this passage, Acts tells us that Paul and Barnabas were both called and commissioned by the Holy Spirit for a special assignment to spread the Gospel far and wide. Scripture says that almost an entire city showed up to hear these men preach. This "special mission" sounds exciting, doesn't it? If you were alive back then, wouldn't you have wanted to be chosen for such a time as this? However, with this great calling came great sacrifice, but isn't this always the case? When we are intentionally living to honor Jesus, we can expect challenges along the way. This was certainly true for Paul and Barnabas.

Scripture says that some people slandered Paul out of jealousy when they saw the large crowds that had come to hear him speak. Paul and Barnabas fought back with the greatest weapon against any vulnerability we have: truth. The Jews didn't like this response and stirred up a mob against them; they figured that since they couldn't silence them, maybe they could run them over. In response, Paul and Barnabas simply moved on to another town with their message. Some of the people who heard them believed and were filled with joy and the Holy Spirit.

This lesson reminds us that God's purposes for us sometimes have a high cost, but it is always worth it. God goes with us as we do the work that He has given us. His power and presence in our lives are all we need.

01 Paul and Barnabas knew that persecution was a part of living obediently to God; this allowed them to not take the rejection they experienced personally. What about you? Do you struggle with holding onto offense?

Do you value what others think about you more than what God thinks about you? Why or why not?

GET RENEWED IN PRAYER

HEY JESUS,

Thank You for choosing to use me to do Your work. Help me to remain sensitive to Your leading. Open my eyes to the people You've placed in front of me who need Your love. Help me say yes to all that You ask of me, even when it feels far outside my comfort zone or beyond my abilities.

Like Paul and Barnabas, show me how to refute lies with truth, opposition with strength, and intimidation with the confidence I find in You. When rejection stings or I feel myself seeking the affirmation of those around me, draw me close. Remind me of what is true and help me keep going. As long as You are with me, I can experience joy and walk in peace wherever I go.

IN JESUS'S NAME, AMEN.

ROMANS 1:16 NLT

For I am not ashamed
of this Good News about Christ.
It is the power of God at work,
saving everyone who believes—
the Jew first and also the Gentile.

GET REMINDED OF TRUTH

GENESIS 3:1–11 NLT

The serpent was the shrewdest of all the wild animals the LORD God had made. One day he asked the woman, "Did God really say you must not eat the fruit from any of the trees in the garden?"

"Of course we may eat fruit from the trees in the garden," the woman replied. "It's only the fruit from the tree in the middle of the garden that we are not allowed to eat. God said, 'You must not eat it or even touch it; if you do, you will die.'"

"You won't die!" the serpent replied to the woman. "God knows that your eyes will be opened as soon as you eat it, and you will be like God, knowing both good and evil."

The woman was convinced. She saw that the tree was beautiful and its fruit looked delicious, and she wanted the wisdom it would give her. So she took some of the fruit and ate it. Then she gave some to her husband, who was with her, and he ate it, too. At that moment their eyes were opened, and they suddenly felt shame at their nakedness. So they sewed fig leaves together to cover themselves.

When the cool evening breezes were blowing, the man and his wife heard the LORD God walking about in the garden. So they hid from the LORD God among the trees. Then the LORD God called to the man, "Where are you?"

He replied, "I heard you walking in the garden, so I hid. I was afraid because I was naked."

"Who told you that you were naked?" the LORD God asked. "Have you eaten from the tree whose fruit I commanded you not to eat?"

SIN THAT LEADS TO SHAME

Is there anything more vulnerable than feeling exposed? Genesis 2:25 tells us that originally, Adam and Eve were naked, but without shame. Their story reminds us that from the beginning of time, vulnerability was a gift from God that later became distorted by the brokenness of sin. How did Satan tempt Eve with the forbidden fruit? Pride. He prompted Eve with the temptation to wonder, "Is God really good? Would He shortchange me?" This tiny doubt about God's character opened the door to disaster. When we meet Adam and Eve in Genesis 3, they are so ashamed of their nakedness that they have made coverings for themselves and attempted to hide from God. That is the result of sin—a desire to run from true vulnerability.

It seems crazy that of all the blessings available to Adam and Eve, they would partake in the one thing God told them to avoid; however, you and I do this every single day. We struggle to trust God's goodness, so we fight for control or pursue pleasure and, in turn, rob ourselves of the ability to live transparently before God and others. But our heavenly Father sent Jesus to redeem this vulnerability—to restore what was lost in the garden, to bring safety and assurance back to our hearts when we unveil our true selves. Ultimately, when we really believe that God is who He says He is, that His promises are true, we are set free to live transparently without shame. We can let down our defenses, knowing that we are provided for and protected every step of the way.

GET REAL WITH YOURSELF

01   Does it make you nervous to think about being fully exposed before God? Do you forget that He knows all already and loves you still?

02   When God asks Adam and Eve, "Where are you?" He wants them to come out from hiding instead of Him finding them. Why do you think this is?

03   Satan can't provide anything good, so his only tactic is to try to make us doubt the goodness of the Father. In which area of your life do you see him do this the most?

GET RENEWED IN PRAYER

HEY JESUS,

How is it that You have given me such a beautiful, wondrous life, and still I doubt Your goodness? And even as I doubt, You cover me. Thank You.

Will You help me recognize when Satan is trying to steal my focus or deter me from walking with You? Reassure me that Your boundary lines for me fall in pleasant places (Psalm 16:6 NIV), protecting my peace, positioning me for success, and preparing me for every step of my journey. Show me how to live a life without shame; You see underneath every defense I raise. I am safe with You, and I don't want to hide anymore.

IN JESUS'S NAME, AMEN.

GALATIANS 4:9 NASB1995

But now that you have come to know God,
or rather to be known by God,
how is it that you turn back again
to the weak and worthless elemental things,
to which you desire to be enslaved all over again?

GET INSPIRED:

Chapter Break Pause

Words that describe who Jesus is and why we can be vulnerable with Him.

```
I E M Z J C A R O I V A S L P R R R P Y
L M Z R C G L N H G W J F F T H T O H I
P L L U T N O Q X G I Y P Y N J M T H R
Y B E A V I E C A E P M U E D I U G Y L
Y C W W O N Y Z T I H P M D K U R R A E
C Z N F B E M X H C Y L F A O E T W I P
X O O Y J T O P R O M I S E N P E Q Q H
C H V V K S A O B H P K P R N U I P K H
O L R E M I P R I N C E F B J I E V E N
L B S B R L R E S T O R E R G L N L F R
L X W D O I T E N I V T R R R N W Z I U
E N D X P B N V C A M O D C E H I Q L F
C R R I Y R U G Z H L K O D M G C K U W
T P A X Q O J X Z E J D R P E P P Z J T
O Q E E B C Q R S M G E E E E R T Z N O
R M W Y T K K N R G H A Y L D A R S W Q
T H E W P B U R C P N A Q L E J U F B T
T A E R G O Z I E X W O B P R A E P R A
Z Z X U C Y T H D A E G Q B P B B D W A
L G N I R P S Y A D N Y S T A R Q P K Z
```

TEAR COLLECTOR	ROCK	REDEEMER
PROMISE KEEPER	PRINCE OF PEACE	RESTORER
GREAT SHEPHERD	ABBA	SAVIOR
COUNSELOR	TRUE VINE	THE WELL
COVERING	IMMANUEL	DAYSPRING
LISTENING EAR	KING	
GUIDE	BREAD OF LIFE	

GET REMINDED OF TRUTH

RUTH 1:3–5, 8–13, 19–21 NLT

Then Elimelech died, and Naomi was left with her two sons. The two sons married Moabite women. One married a woman named Orpah, and the other a woman named Ruth. But about ten years later, both Mahlon and Kilion died. This left Naomi alone, without her two sons or her husband.
...

But on the way, Naomi said to her two daughters-in-law, "Go back to your mothers' homes. And may the LORD reward you for your kindness to your husbands and to me. May the LORD bless you with the security of another marriage." Then she kissed them good-bye, and they all broke down and wept.

"No," they said. "We want to go with you to your people."

But Naomi replied, "Why should you go on with me? Can I still give birth to other sons who could grow up to be your husbands? No,

my daughters, return to your parents' homes, for I am too old to marry again. And even if it were possible, and I were to get married tonight and bear sons, then what? Would you wait for them to grow up and refuse to marry someone else? No, of course not, my daughters! Things are far more bitter for me than for you, because the LORD Himself has raised His fist against me." ...

So the two of them continued on their journey. When they came to Bethlehem, the entire town was excited by their arrival. "Is it really Naomi?" the women asked.

"Don't call me Naomi," she responded. "Instead, call me Mara, for the Almighty has made life very bitter for me. I went away full, but the LORD has brought me home empty. Why call me Naomi when the LORD has caused me to suffer and the Almighty has sent such tragedy upon me?"

GET CANDID WITH CLEERE

WHEN TRAGEDY MAKES YOU BITTER

Naomi had lost her husband and both sons in ten years' time. Full of grief, anger, and bitterness, Naomi felt like her life had been stolen from her. When she and her daughter-in-law, Ruth, traveled back to Naomi's home village, everyone questioned whether it was Naomi returning, knowing that she had not returned since the death of her family. In response, Naomi redefined herself as "Mara," which means "bitter." She wanted to be called this name because she said, "the Almighty has made [my] life very bitter" (Ruth 1:20).

Grief has a way of clouding our judgment, doesn't it? When we are drowning in sorrow, it feels too difficult to lift our heads and see our blessings. It seems easier to call things a loss and hang it up or quit. I think God welcomes our bitterness, grief, and anguish. He feels it with us—deeper than we ever could because He made us. But then, He pulls us out of the pit and helps us embrace hope again. Personally, I think that's why God provided Ruth to Naomi: He wanted to physically remind her, "I know you don't think I see you, but you are not alone. I know you feel lost." The hard thing about really sad experiences is that the new normal will never be the old normal. However, the best is always ahead of us when we follow Jesus. Naomi may have stamped herself "Mara," but God reidentified her: "Mine."

GET REAL WITH YOURSELF

01 As social media allows us continual exposure to the events all around us, do you think it's easy to be bitter about the harshness of the world and the bad things that happen? Why or why not?

02 Has there ever been a time in your life when things have happened and you wondered, "God, why did You do this to me? Why have you made me this way?" Did He meet you there? Explain.

03 Later in the book of Ruth, Ruth finds a faithful husband in Boaz, and Naomi becomes part of the lineage of Jesus. Their new normal was different than the old one, but beautiful. How have you seen God bring things full circle in your own life?

GET RENEWED IN PRAYER

HEY JESUS,

Thank You for the way that You bend down to listen to every prayer in my heart. You aren't angry with me because I am struggling; You grieve with me, yearning to mend my heart so that I can see life as You see it. Thank You for helping me recognize my bitterness. Open my eyes to all that remains good in my life and lead me back to peace. When I want my old normal back, give me fresh eyes and anticipation for how You are using my current circumstances.

Father, remind me that no matter how heavy and dark my emotions feel, that they are not my identity. You say that I am Yours. This helps me find joy in the chaos, strength in the struggle, and peace when nothing makes sense. Help me praise Your name in all things because You are always worthy. Sorrow may last for the night, but joy comes in the morning (Psalm 30:5).

IN JESUS'S NAME, AMEN.

HEBREWS 12:14–15 ESV

Strive for peace with everyone,
and for the holiness without which no one will see the Lord.
See to it that no one fails to obtain the grace of God;
that no "root of bitterness" springs up and causes trouble,
and by it many become defiled.

GET REMINDED OF TRUTH

LUKE 18:11–12 NLT

[Then Jesus told this story]: "The Pharisee stood by himself and prayed this prayer: 'I thank You, God, that I am not like other people—cheaters, sinners, adulterers. I'm certainly not like that tax collector! I fast twice a week, and I give You a tenth of my income.'"

LUKE 19:1–10 NLT

Jesus entered Jericho and made His way through the town. There was a man there named Zacchaeus. He was the chief tax collector in the region, and he had become very rich. He tried to get a look at Jesus, but he was too short to see over the crowd. So he ran ahead and climbed a sycamore-fig tree beside the road, for Jesus was going to pass that way.

When Jesus came by, He looked up at Zacchaeus and called him by name.

"Zacchaeus!" He said. "Quick, come down! I must be a guest in your home today."

Zacchaeus quickly climbed down and took Jesus to his house in great excitement and joy. But the people were displeased. "He has gone to be the guest of a notorious sinner," they grumbled.

Meanwhile, Zacchaeus stood before the Lord and said, "I will give half my wealth to the poor, Lord, and if I have cheated people on their taxes, I will give them back four times as much!"

Jesus responded, "Salvation has come to this home today, for this man has shown himself to be a true son of Abraham. For the Son of Man came to seek and save those who are lost."

CHANGE OF HEART

During this time, tax collectors were hated by their fellow Israelites for their thieving ways; they are often mentioned in Scripture in regard to their relationships with Jesus. He sought them out. Made friends with them. And both Zacchaeus and Levi responded to Jesus's love and mercy with repentance and devotion.

In this passage, Zacchaeus (known to be a very short man) climbed a tree so he could hear the teachings of Jesus as He preached. His expectant heart proved the transformation that had begun to take place inside of him. Jesus knew the stirring that was happening inside Zacchaeus and responded by seeking him out. He ordered Zacchaeus to come down from the tree so that He could accompany him to his home for a visit. Jesus was aware of the tax collector's bad reputation, but it didn't stop Him from associating with him. Jesus wanted the crowds that followed Him to know that His love and restoration were available to everyone, no matter their past.

God is always ready to welcome us home—arms open, no record of wrongs, just as we are.

The name Zacchaeus means "pure" or "innocent." When Jesus sought Zacchaeus out, He was reminding him of who he truly was, not who he had become through a series of destructive choices. Zacchaeus responded by offering to repay others far more than he had taken from them. The love and grace of Jesus changed him.

This is the power of coming to Jesus with our mistakes and failures—He is able to redeem and restore us to better than ever before with no questions asked.

GET REAL WITH YOURSELF

01   If you're honest, it's sometimes frustrating when others experience God's blessings despite their poor choices, isn't it? How does the story of Zacchaeus challenge your heart in this way?

02   Jesus could have just responded to Zacchaeus and told him He forgave him for his past and just kept on preaching. Instead, He insisted on going to Zacchaeus's home. Why do you think that is?

03   Do you believe there are parts of you or your story that disqualify you from being a true child of God or receiving the benefits of your God-given identity? Why or why not?

GET RENEWED IN PRAYER

HEY JESUS,

Thank You for the way that You see me—through Your eyes, I am blameless and pure. Kind and gracious. Loved and set free because of You. Help me see my life, and the world, through Your eyes. Give the courage to break free from the comforts of my lifestyle that don't please You. You don't label me by my mistakes or even my gifts; You identify me as Your child.

As I interact with others, remind me of this truth. Give me Your love for others, desiring redemption and blessing for their lives instead of consequence and retaliation. Grace is Your free gift for every heart, including mine. When I witness Your mercy for others, help me celebrate Your faithfulness.

IN JESUS'S NAME, AMEN.

Revelation 3:20 NLT

"Look! I stand at the door and knock.
If you hear My voice and open the door,
I will come in, and we will share a meal together as friends."

Chapter Break Pause

Take time to think through each Scripture, and then select two for memorization.
The next time your emotions start to run wild,
recall these verses to mind and anchor yourself in their comforting truths.

*Draw near to God, and he will
draw near to you. Cleanse your hands,
you sinners, and purify your hearts, you
double-minded. Be wretched and mourn
and weep. Let your laughter be turned to
mourning and your joy to gloom. Humble
yourselves before the Lord,
and he will exalt you.*

JAMES 4:8–10 ESV

*Don't worry about anything;
instead, pray about everything.
Tell God what you need, and thank Him
for all He has done. Then you will experience
God's peace, which exceeds anything we
can understand. His peace will guard your
hearts and minds as you live in Christ Jesus.*

PHILIPPIANS 4:6–7 NLT

*For the mind set on the flesh is death, but the
mind set on the Spirit is life and peace.*

ROMANS 8:6 NASB1995

*We are destroying speculations and every
lofty thing raised up against the knowledge
of God, and we are taking every thought
captive to the obedience of Christ.*

II CORINTHIANS 10:5 NASB1995

*In view of all this, make every effort to
respond to God's promises. Supplement
your faith with a generous provision of
moral excellence, and moral excellence with
knowledge, and knowledge with self-control,
and self-control with patient endurance,
and patient endurance with godliness, and
godliness with brotherly affection, and
brotherly affection with love for everyone.*

II PETER 1:5–7 NLT

*Therefore, put on every piece of God's armor
so you will be able to resist the enemy in the
time of evil. Then after the battle you will
still be standing firm. Stand your ground,
putting on the belt of truth and the body
armor of God's righteousness. For shoes,
put on the peace that comes from the Good
News so that you will be fully prepared. In
addition to all of these, hold up the shield of
faith to stop the fiery arrows of the devil. Put
on salvation as your helmet, and take the
sword of the Spirit, which is the word of God.*

EPHESIANS 6:13–17 NLT

*"Know this, my beloved brothers:
let every person be quick to hear,
slow to speak, slow to anger;
for the anger of man does not produce
the righteousness of God."*

JAMES 1:19–20 ESV

*Therefore, preparing your minds for action,
and being sober-minded, set your hope fully
on the grace that will be brought to you at
the revelation of Jesus Christ.*

I PETER 1:13 ESV

*A person without self-control is like a city
with broken-down walls.*

PROVERBS 25:28 NLT

*Submit yourselves therefore to God.
Resist the devil, and he will flee from you.*

JAMES 4:7 ESV

GET REMINDED OF TRUTH

ESTHER 4:1–3, 10–17 NLT

When Mordecai learned about all that had been done, he tore his clothes, put on burlap and ashes, and went out into the city, crying with a loud and bitter wail. He went as far as the gate of the palace, for no one was allowed to enter the palace gate while wearing clothes of mourning. And as news of the king's decree reached all the provinces, there was great mourning among the Jews. They fasted, wept, and wailed, and many people lay in burlap and ashes. ...

Then Esther told Hathach to go back and relay this message to Mordecai: "All the king's officials and even the people in the provinces know that anyone who appears before the king in his inner court without being invited is doomed to die unless the king holds out his gold scepter. And the king has not called

for me to come to him for thirty days." So Hathach gave Esther's message to Mordecai.

Mordecai sent this reply to Esther: "Don't think for a moment that because you're in the palace you will escape when all other Jews are killed. If you keep quiet at a time like this, deliverance and relief for the Jews will arise from some other place, but you and your relatives will die. Who knows if perhaps you were made queen for just such a time as this?"

Then Esther sent this reply to Mordecai: "Go and gather together all the Jews of Susa and fast for me. Do not eat or drink for three days, night or day. My maids and I will do the same. And then, though it is against the law, I will go in to see the king. If I must die, I must die." So Mordecai went away and did everything as Esther had ordered him.

GET CANDID WITH CLEERE

ELEVATED TO SERVE

Receiving the crown always sounds so glamorous and enticing, doesn't it? Queen Esther was the beautiful, esteemed queen to Xerxes, King of Persia. Although Esther was Jewish, she had not told anyone in the royal court of her family lineage or nationality. The reason why this is such a crazy detail is because during this time, Haman (King Xerxes's chief advisor), made a plot to kill all the Jews (Esther 3) because Mordecai (Esther's relative who took care of her growing up) refused to bow down to him. The dramatic turn of events ends up putting Esther in the most vulnerable position: Will she sacrifice her security to save her people? Will she risk her own death to preserve the lives of others?

The story continues with unpredictable twists and turns, but the Jewish people end up being saved, Haman is killed, and Mordecai becomes the prime minister next to Xerxes. It sounds like a happy ending, but the truth is, risking our safety in the service of others is terrifying. This story reminds us that God often positions us (like Mordecai being positioned as Esther's guardian and then Esther being positioned in the palace) to play a part in His plan to redeem and heal His people. Mordecai's vulnerability with Esther helped open her eyes to the possibility that perhaps she was made for such a time as this (Esther 4:14). The crown will feel heavy at times, but when we realize the pressure is on God to save like only He can, we find the strength to show up where we are.

GET REAL WITH YOURSELF

01   Reflect on a time when you felt a sense of fear or hesitation in risking your own safety or comfort for the well-being of others. How did you navigate that fear, and what did you learn from the experience?

02   In what ways do you see God positioning people in your life, or perhaps yourself, to play a part in His plan to bring healing and redemption to those around you?

03   Is there a time in your life where you were elevated to a place that required more from you than you realized? Write about it.

GET RENEWED IN PRAYER

HEY JESUS,

Thank You for calling me and caring for me in every season. I walk with confidence knowing that wherever I am, You have equipped me to thrive in that space. Help me realize that the gifts You have given me, the opportunities You have afforded me, and the resources with which You have blessed me are not just for my benefit, but for those around me.

Thank You for providing me with people around me who tell me the truth and keep me accountable. Give me discernment to know which voices are true. When I find myself fearing man over You, guide me back to worship where I remember that You're sovereign over everything. All is in Your hands. Like Esther, give me the courage to fulfill Your plans for my life, entrusting everything I have to You.

IN JESUS'S NAME, AMEN.

PHILIPPIANS 2:13 NASB1995

For it is God who is at work in you,
both to will and to work for His good pleasure.

GET REMINDED OF TRUTH

NUMBERS 12:1–13 NLT

While they were at Hazeroth, Miriam and Aaron criticized Moses because he had married a Cushite woman. They said, "Has the LORD spoken only through Moses? Hasn't He spoken through us, too?" But the LORD heard them. (Now Moses was very humble—more humble than any other person on earth.)

So immediately the LORD called to Moses, Aaron, and Miriam and said, "Go out to the Tabernacle, all three of you!" So the three of them went to the Tabernacle. Then the LORD descended in the pillar of cloud and stood at the entrance of the Tabernacle. "Aaron and Miriam!" He called, and they stepped forward. And the LORD said to them, "Now listen to what I say: 'If there were prophets among you, I, the LORD, would reveal Myself in visions. I would speak to them in dreams. But not with My servant Moses. Of all My house, he is the one I trust. I speak to him face to face, clearly, and not in riddles! He sees the LORD as He is. So why were you not afraid to criticize My servant Moses?"

The LORD was very angry with them, and He departed. As the cloud moved from above the Tabernacle, there stood Miriam, her skin as white as snow from leprosy. When Aaron saw what had happened to her, he cried out to Moses, "Oh, my master! Please don't punish us for this sin we have so foolishly committed. Don't let her be like a stillborn baby, already decayed at birth."

So Moses cried out to the LORD, 'O God, I beg You, please heal her!'"

GET CANDID WITH CLEERE

WHEN COMPARISON LEADS TO CRITICISM

Miriam was strong, bold, and courageous. She was Moses's older sister who helped, alongside their brother Aaron, lead the Israelites to the Promised Land. Referenced in the Bible as a "prophetess," she was one of the few women to receive that title. However, I think it's helpful when we realize that these incredible people throughout Scripture experienced moments where they doubted the goodness and wisdom of God. In this passage, Miriam and Aaron criticized Moses for marrying a Cushite woman, but the deeper motivation of their hearts was revealed in the question, "Has the Lord spoken only through Moses? Hasn't He spoken through us, too?" They had fallen into the trap of pride. This prompted them to trust their own insight over God's wisdom, further leading to destruction. That's what pride does— it invites a critical spirit that puts us on a pedestal upon which we can't survive, making us vulnerable to falling into temptation.

The Lord responded with punishment, covering Miriam in leprosy. This feels harsh, doesn't it? However, I think the Lord wanted to teach a strong lesson: when we compare ourselves or our assignments to others, we are doubting God's wisdom and authority.

There is redemption in this story, though. Moses interceded with God for his sister, Miriam was cured, and they continued forward. This prophetess was reminded that God's wisdom is always best and that she could trust His choices.

GET REAL WITH YOURSELF

01   Reflect on a time when you found yourself questioning or doubting God's wisdom in a situation. What were the consequences, if any?

02   Pride often leads to a critical spirit, as seen in Miriam and Aaron's questioning of Moses. How do you guard against pride in your own life, and what practices help you remain humble before God's wisdom?

03   Consider moments when you've compared yourself or your circumstances to others. How did this comparison impact your trust in God's wisdom and authority?

GET RENEWED IN PRAYER

HEY JESUS,

Thank You for committing to my inner transformation and the deep work of my heart, whatever it requires. I'm grateful that You're always preparing me for what's next. Will You help me remember that any success I achieve is always because Your hand is holding me and helping me?

Like Miriam, sometimes I want to ask You why others are promoted, or I struggle with comparing myself to those around me, wondering if You've forgotten me or think less of me. I know that You hear me, even when I feel like You're silent. Remind me that Your ways are unpredictable, but they are always trustworthy. When I am tempted to behave critically of others in order to elevate myself, give me fresh perspective. Reassure me that a victory for anyone who is serving You is a victory for everyone. Help me resist pride as You strengthen me in Your promises.

IN JESUS'S NAME, AMEN.

I PETER 2:1–3 NIV

Therefore, rid yourselves of all malice and all deceit,
hypocrisy, envy, and slander of every kind.
Like newborn babies, crave pure spiritual milk,
so that by it you may grow up in your salvation,
now that you have tasted that the Lord is good.

Chapter Break Pause

Explore these Scriptures and pick two for memorization.
When others need a safe space to be vulnerable,
draw upon these verses in your mind.

But encourage one another daily, as long as it is called 'Today,'
so that none of you may be hardened by sin's deceitfulness.
HEBREWS 3:13 NIV

"Rejoice with those who rejoice, and weep with those who weep."
ROMANS 12:15 NKJV

Since God chose you to be the holy people He loves, you must clothe yourselves with
tenderhearted mercy, kindness, humility, gentleness, and patience.
COLOSSIANS 3:12 NLT

Therefore encourage one another and build one another up, just as you are doing.
I THESSALONIANS 5:11 ESV

Bear one another's burdens, and so fulfill the law of Christ.
GALATIANS 6:2 ESV

Love one another with brotherly affection. Outdo one another in showing honor.
ROMANS 12:10 ESV

Therefore, confess your sins to one another and pray for one another, that you may be
healed. The prayer of a righteous person has great power as it is working.
JAMES 5:16 ESV

Finally, all of you, have unity of mind, sympathy, brotherly love,
a tender heart, and a humble mind.
I PETER 3:8 ESV

Let no corrupting talk come out of your mouths, but only such as is good for building up,
as fits the occasion, that it may give grace to those who hear.
EPHESIANS 4:29 ESV

Therefore let us not pass judgment on one another any longer, but rather decide never
to put a stumbling block or hindrance in the way of a brother.
ROMANS 14:13 ESV

GET REMINDED OF TRUTH

GENESIS 25:23–34 NLT

And the Lord *told her, "The sons in your womb will become two nations. From the very beginning, the two nations will be rivals. One nation will be stronger than the other; and your older son will serve your younger son."*

And when the time came to give birth, Rebekah discovered that she did indeed have twins! The first one was very red at birth and covered with thick hair like a fur coat. So they named him Esau. Then the other twin was born with his hand grasping Esau's heel. So they named him Jacob. Isaac was sixty years old when the twins were born.

As the boys grew up, Esau became a skillful hunter. He was an outdoorsman, but Jacob had a quiet temperament, preferring to stay at home. Isaac loved Esau because he enjoyed eating the wild game Esau brought home, but Rebekah loved Jacob.

One day when Jacob was cooking some stew, Esau arrived home from the wilderness exhausted and hungry. Esau said to Jacob, "I'm starved! Give me some of that red stew!" (This is how Esau got his other name, Edom, which means "red.")

"All right," Jacob replied, "but trade me your rights as the firstborn son."

"Look, I'm dying of starvation!" said Esau. "What good is my birthright to me now?"

But Jacob said, "First you must swear that your birthright is mine." So Esau swore an oath, thereby selling all his rights as the firstborn to his brother, Jacob.

Then Jacob gave Esau some bread and lentil stew. Esau ate the meal, then got up and left. He showed contempt for his rights as the firstborn.

GET CANDID WITH CLEERE

STARVED OF PERSPECTIVE

It is difficult to understand why Esau might sell his birth rights as the firstborn son to his brother, Jacob, simply because he was hungry and needed some soup. How could he trade something that determined so much of his future for something that only affected his next few hours?

In truth, however, Esau's weakness in this story is something you and I struggle with too. Sometimes, without even realizing it, we begin to invest in temporary things for the fleeting pleasure they provide at the cost of those that will last for eternity.

But Esau wasn't the only brother at fault here. Jacob also chose the immediate gratification over something far more precious: his character. Jacob didn't hesitate to manipulate his own brother for the sake of his personal gain. Sadly, Jacob isn't alone in this. We often put others in adverse situations so that we can have the advantage.

In both men's stories, God reminds us that when we consume ourselves with the temporary, we become vulnerable to making choices that are dishonoring to Him and hurtful to others. May He grant us the wisdom, and self-control, to make better choices.

GET REAL WITH YOURSELF

01   Reflect on a time when you, like Esau, were tempted to prioritize temporary satisfaction over long-term consequences. How did that choice impact your life and relationships?

02   Jacob's actions highlight the temptation to manipulate others for personal gain. In what ways have you observed or experienced similar behaviors in yourself or others? How can one guard against such tendencies?

03   Jacob struggled to trust God's plan throughout his life even though God was faithful to provide for him. Make a list below of the ways God has met your needs in the past. Thank Him for each of them. Keep them handy and refer to them when you feel doubtful.

GET RENEWED IN PRAYER

HEY JESUS,

Thank You for the constant reminder to keep the long game in mind. I know that an eternal perspective protects my peace, helps me keep my priorities straight, and provides me with true security. Like Esau, I am sometimes tempted to satisfy my temporary desires because they feel so pressing. Can you help me control my emotions and remind me that You provide for my needs? Show me how to choose contentment when I don't get what I want when I want it.

When I feel the urge to take matters into my own hands or manipulate others like Jacob, nudge my spirit. In You, I find the perseverance, hope, and strength I need to live faithfully.

IN JESUS'S NAME, AMEN.

COLOSSIANS 3:2 NASB1995

Set your mind on the things above,
not on the things that are on earth.

GET REMINDED OF TRUTH

MARK 14:32–42 NLT

They went to the olive grove called Gethsemane, and Jesus said, "Sit here while I go and pray." He took Peter, James, and John with Him, and He became deeply troubled and distressed. He told them, "My soul is crushed with grief to the point of death. Stay here and keep watch with Me."

He went on a little farther and fell to the ground. He prayed that, if it were possible, the awful hour awaiting Him might pass Him by. "Abba, Father," He cried out, "everything is possible for You. Please take this cup of suffering away from Me. Yet I want Your will to be done, not Mine."

Then He returned and found the disciples asleep. He said to Peter, "Simon, are you asleep? Couldn't you watch with Me even one hour? Keep watch and pray, so that you will not give in to temptation. For the spirit is willing, but the body is weak."

Then Jesus left them again and prayed the same prayer as before. When He returned to them again, He found them sleeping, for they couldn't keep their eyes open. And they didn't know what to say.

When He returned to them the third time, He said, "Go ahead and sleep. Have your rest. But no—the time has come. The Son of Man is betrayed into the hands of sinners. Up, let's be going. Look, My betrayer is here!"

WILLING BUT AFRAID

Jesus, the Savior of the world, prayed this prayer, "Abba, Father, everything is possible for You. Please take this cup of suffering away from Me." The cross was not a surprise for Him, but that didn't change how He felt about having to endure it: full of grief, anguish, and sorrow. It's chilling to read that the most powerful, loving, and capable person who ever walked the earth spent moments crying out to His Father, asking to be spared. Surely, God could do it—there is nothing He can't—would He save Him and provide another way?

In my heart of hearts, I think Jesus knew what He had to do, but it was still terrifying. The stress of what was ahead of Him caused Him to sweat blood. I believe Scripture includes details like this to help us understand that every emotion, all our deepest fears, and everything we wish wasn't true for our lives—Jesus gets it. The depth of His grief didn't shortchange the devotion of His soul. "Yet I want Your will to be done, not Mine" is how Jesus concluded His prayer—allowing Himself to express His emotions, while in the same breath, realizing that His feelings may not align with the Father's will.

Jesus's struggle reminds us that the body is weak, but God is strong, and His sovereign will can withstand every emotion we experience.

GET REAL WITH YOURSELF

01   Reflect on a time when you faced a challenging situation and found yourself wrestling with your emotions while simultaneously surrendering to God's will. How did that experience shape your understanding of prayer and surrender?

02   Consider the idea that Jesus, despite being fully aware of His mission, expressed genuine grief, anguish, and sorrow. How does knowing that Jesus experienced these deep emotions resonate with your own struggles and challenges?

03   Jesus's prayer in the garden reveals His humanity and vulnerability. In what ways does understanding Jesus's emotional experience during this pivotal moment draw you closer to Him and help you connect with your own emotions in prayer?

GET RENEWED IN PRAYER

HEY JESUS,

Thank You for being You. Even in the darkest, most difficult circumstance any human heart could ever face, Your character was consistent. Your willingness to go to the cross for me, despite my sin, will never be lost on me.

Thank You for empathizing with my feelings of "I wish this wasn't my story." Knowing that You had moments when You dreaded what was before You brings me great relief and comfort.

When I am in distress, help me take time away to process how I feel, just like You did. Help me find quiet so that I can hear You and let You restore me.

You endured the greatest suffering, and yet, You counted it all joy. You knew the end, and therefore, You found perseverance for the in-between; remind me that my ultimate destination is heaven forever with You so that I can do the same.

IN JESUS'S NAME, AMEN.

MATTHEW 27:46 ESV

And about the ninth hour Jesus
cried out with a loud voice, saying,
"Eli, Eli, lema sabachthani?" that is,
"My God, my God, why have you forsaken me?"

Want more from Cleere?

You can find her devotionals and
Prayers to Share on dayspring.com,
as well as several retail stores near you.

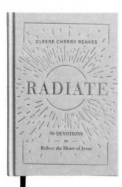

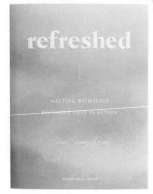

CLEERE CHERRY REAVES is the owner and creator of *Cleerely Stated*, a successful business that started with a simple blog and turned into a full product line that can be found online and in retail stores all over the United States. Well-known for her easy-to-relate-to, practical writing style, Cleere's mission is to help others see themselves and the world around them through the eyes of Jesus. Cleere now hosts a growing podcast called *Let's Be Cleere*, where she hopes people are encouraged by the raw, real love of Jesus. She was born and raised in Greenville, North Carolina. She's a proud alumnus of the University of North Carolina at Chapel Hill and loves to live life to the fullest.

Dear Friend,

This book was prayerfully crafted with you, the reader, in mind. Every word, every sentence, every page was thoughtfully written, designed, and packaged to encourage you—right where you are this very moment. At DaySpring, our vision is to see every person experience the life-changing message of God's love. So, as we worked through rough drafts, design changes, edits, and details, we prayed for you to deeply experience His unfailing love, indescribable peace, and pure joy. It is our sincere hope that through these Truth-filled pages your heart will be blessed, knowing that God cares about you—your desires and disappointments, your challenges and dreams.

He knows. He cares. He loves you unconditionally.

BLESSINGS!
THE DAYSPRING BOOK TEAM

Additional copies of this book and
other DaySpring titles can be purchased
at fine retailers everywhere.
Order online at <u>dayspring.com</u>
or
by phone at 1-877-751-4347

Written by: Cleere Cherry Reaves
Cover Design by: Becca Barnett

Printed in China
Prime: U1868
ISBN: 979-8-88602-549-1